The Japanese Are Like That

Ichiro Kawasaki

The Japanese

are LIKE THAT

CHARLES E. TUTTLE COMPANY
Rutland, Vermont   Tokyo, Japan

Representatives
Continental Europe: BOXERBOOKS, INC., *Zurich*
British Isles: PRENTICE-HALL INTERNATIONAL, INC., *London*
Australasia: PAUL FLESCH & CO., PTY. LTD., *Melbourne*
Canada: HURTIG PUBLISHERS, *Edmonton*

Published by the Charles E. Tuttle Co., Inc.
of Rutland, Vermont and Tokyo, Japan
with editorial offices at Suido 1-chome, 2-6
Bunkyo-ku, Tokyo

Library of Congress Catalog Card No. 55-10620

International Standard Book No. 0-8048-0281-5

First edition, June 1955
Twenty-third printing, 1975

0339-000154-4615

Printed in Japan

Contents

Contents

Author's Preface

THE Japan of the gorgeous cherry blossoms, the beautiful geisha, and the sublime Mt. Fuji has been told and retold in a thousand and one books published throughout the world during the past century. But this is not the real Japan with which the rest of the present-day world is vitally concerned. The Japan which the world must come to know is the new Japan, the reborn Japan. When I say reborn, I am contrasting the new Japan with that Japan which rose meteorically from an Oriental, historic obscurity to rank as one of the world's foremost powers, which rocked the whole world for several years with a fanatical war, to be finally laid prostrate by a catastrophic defeat, the first in its long history. The reborn Japan of which I speak starts perhaps at the same point at which it found itself more than a half-century ago, and only by understanding this new Japan can one hope to predict its future course.

The point of view from which I discuss the ways of life of the Japanese is in terms of contrasts with those of other countries where I have had some personal experience. My remarks do not deal directly with great world problems; it is my opinion that the needs and desires of the Japanese will be better understood by other peoples if they see us as we actually live from day to day. If the world is to move in the direction of harmony, it will have to move in terms of a more realistic understanding between one people and another. By understanding, I do not necessarily mean sympathy; I refer instead to a knowledge and perhaps appreciation of the cultural background of a people and a realization that this cultural background is a living force from which no people can escape and which indeed prevents them from reforming themselves as fast as they might wish.

I have done my best to portray the customs and habits of my countrymen in an objective light. I am fully aware that I am exposing myself to criticism for showing their shortcomings in too glaring a light. As I see it, however, my task is to paint a picture of Japan today just as it is. On the other hand, since we Japanese cannot be our own judges, I attempt no critical appraisal—this task, pleasant or unpleasant, is for the rest of the world.

It is my most sincere desire that both foreigners and Japanese will weigh carefully what I have written and will gain some benefit thereby. I hope that other lands will gain a clearer understanding of "what sort of people" the Japanese really are and that my discussion of some of their more lamentable characteristics will contribute to more realistic thinking about Japan.

Finally, I like to hope that this book may bring one step closer to reality my dream of a world of tolerance and justice where the citizens of all countries will be able to make the rounds, freely and in friendship, not only of their neighbors' lands, but of their neighbors' neighbors' lands as well.

Tokyo, Japan   Ichiro Kawasaki
June, 1955

1 A Japanese Rip van Winkle in America

ONE morning in 1950 while sitting in my office discussing a measure which, at the suggestion of the Occupation authorities, was to be undertaken by the local Japanese government, I was summoned by my superior. Carefully collecting my papers together, I mentally tabulated all our ideas on the measure at hand and went into my bureau chief's office. I was prepared to relate as best I could the analysis of the measure and the means by which I thought it could best be put into operation. My chief, with a document in his hand, motioned me to sit down, which I did.

Looking at the document which he held, he related its contents to me: "On the basis of our careful recommendation, the General Headquarters

11

has approved a mission to the United States which you are to head, and has already determined the time of departure of your mission." He went on to explain that some fifteen representatives of various offices in prefectures, cities, towns, and villages would make a three month's tour of the United States and visit various specified cities. We would carry out intensive research in each locality, which it was hoped would enable us to bring back to Japan useful knowledge of the workings of state and local governments in the United States. By means of such tours, even though of short duration, my superior went on to say, General MacArthur desired that as many Japanese officials as possible should observe representative government in action. We were to observe democratic principles and practices as Americans used them. He gave me a list of the offices which were to be represented and stated that in a day or so I would meet the delegates chosen to represent those offices. He congratulated me on having been assigned to head the mission and teasingly told me that he was slightly jealous for not going in my place.

Have you ever been taken back with surprise or "rocked," as my English friends say? I expressed my deepest gratitude as well as I could and gathered my papers awkwardly from the chair and floor to which they had fallen. I was indeed surprised and overjoyed at the appointment, and the details of the measure I had so carefully prepared floated away in my excitement.

I left his office and departed for home, without

a word to any of my associates, even though they eyed me inquiringly. I was deeply happy that I was going to the United States once again, regardless of the mission. Today, I am happy that I went, and I shall continue to be the rest of my life.

I was so anxious to start that it seemed to take an eternity for the members of the mission to assemble! As the other members arrived on successive days, I discovered that they too were excited and anxious to take off. Just as my superior had informed me, these fellow delegates came from all parts of Japan. There was Governor S. from Kyushu, the southernmost island of the country, who was anxious above all else to learn the workings of state assemblies in America. Mr. K., who had served many years as a prefectural governor both in Japan and Korea, wanted to know how excise-tax revenues were collected in American municipalities. Mayor S. of a town in Aichi prefecture was eager to study garbage disposal and fly extermination in various rural municipalities in the United States. Then there was Mr. I., until recently Vice-Minister of Education in Tokyo, who was interested in school districts of America, a subject about which the Japanese were almost totally ignorant.

Before we had too much time to express our impatience, we found ourselves actually flying along 20,000 feet over the enormous expanse of the Pacific. The conversation of my immediate companions and the little chats I had with the others aboard gave me pause for serious contemplation. Here we were

13

speeding to the United States, and none of my companions had ever been there before. "What did they expect?" I wondered.

On board the great Pan-American clipper soon after leaving Tokyo, we were each given a carton containing various kinds of food, including a big piece of roast chicken! My fellow passengers asked me in whispered tones whether this constituted the whole day's ration. What a surprise we had when we were told that that was to be our breakfast and that we would be fed similarly at each mealtime! Having been used for so many years to meager food supplies, especially during the war years, we naturally reveled in this American extravagance. What we used to get occasionally at first-class restaurants in our country and thought was a sumptuous repast was but "chicken feed" in comparison.

In my travels to various countries while I was an official with the Foreign Office of the Imperial Japanese Government, I was often profoundly shocked by certain customs of the people in those countries. I was jerked around more than once by the structure of their language in terms of mine. It is my opinion that what some of my foreign friends regard as merely trivial become more often than not the monumental hurdles in otherwise peaceful journeys. These minor customs, methods of speaking or thinking or acting, so frequently become the turning points of truly great issues that all of them deserve more than a casual survey. As for myself, I have studied them as best I can.

Thus, though coming to the United States with a group of my countrymen on an important mission, my thoughts and interests turned to the little habits and customs of daily living. I could picture our group being most curious and even amused by what we observed and also could see that, even though my companions spoke and understood little English, they realized that they themselves would be the cause for many an American to chuckle.

While thus musing, I resolved, in touring about America this time, to draw as many comparisons as I could. My companions had already given me evidence of a similar desire on their part, and throughout the entire journey, I was never surprised to see them making quick but lengthy entries in their fattening notebooks. Our primary concern would be: How do Americans do things? Moreover, for us Japanese the question does not cover just a few things, it includes everything! But we had little time for philosophizing! We were landing!

As our giant trans-Pacific clipper roared over the Bay region of California in the early morning and headed toward Travis Airfield, memories came back thick and fast of my residence in San Francisco a decade before.

Thoughts of Tokyo, left behind only thirty-seven hours before, were rapidly receding into haziness, and others raced into our excited minds! I had thought Tokyo was a prosperous metropolis, whose war scars had finally been obliterated; some foreign visitors have called our city the "oasis of the troubled

Orient." As a matter of fact, as we took off from Haneda Airport and soared over the twin-city area of Tokyo and Yokohama two nights before, I had been impressed by the myriads of glittering lights beneath us, which presented a veritable fairyland! I flattered myself that my country was well on its way to recovery and imagined that neither San Francisco nor New York would look different from Tokyo when viewed from the air at night. My illusions were rudely shattered, for here below me was this great city, whose powerful incandescent lamps lit up imposing skyscrapers and showed block after block of homes and buildings in clear relief. Tokyo is a compactly built-up area with seven and one-half million people. But how dim Tokyo seemed in comparison!

Soon after our arrival at the California airdrome, one of the first sights to greet our eyes was the constant stream of motor vehicles on the highway leading to San Francisco. What a sight to behold! That wriggling stream was a never-ending procession of shining limousines and monstrous vans racing along on the six-lane highway. It was stupendous, breath-taking, and almost unbelievable.

Tokyo today abounds in automobiles—we have more cars on the roads now than we had in the most prosperous prewar years. Narrow and straggling Tokyo streets have almost become untenable with some 60,000 passenger cars. The city of Tokyo has a population of some seven and a half million, so the ratio of automobiles to population is one car for every

16

125 persons. In contrast, we were told that the ratio in California was one car for every two persons. A dusty concrete and macadam road links Tokyo and Yokohama and constitutes Japan's Route 1 national highway. Compared with this cavalcade, however, it seemed like a mere country lane.

As I rode into San Francisco, all the buildings seemed massive and awe-inspiring. True, we have eight- to ten-story reinforced-concrete buildings everywhere in Tokyo, Kyoto, Kobe, Osaka, and Nagoya, and still more are being built. But how undersized they are in Western terms! Our ten-story buildings are no higher than a four-story building of the same kind of steel and concrete structure in America. Ours are smaller in scale in almost every respect, especially in the height of the rooms. Likewise, sidewalks of the city streets in the United States are perhaps three times wider than those of the Ginza, Tokyo's Fifth Avenue. Also, the streets are less crowded, and people seem to breathe more freely in the United States. In suburban districts, especially, this sense of space is particularly in evidence. Nowhere in Japan can be found such spacious lawns as are seen on American university campuses. Even the patches of small lawns which surround most middle-class duplex homes are seldom, if ever, duplicated in the urban areas of my country.

One day while in San Francisco, I went to see the house in which I and my family had lived some ten years ago. How spacious and spick-and-span the house looked! Having been plunged right into the

17

abundance and affluence of America from war-torn and congested Japan, the contrast was indeed striking. I could hardly believe my eyes. Yet, as I thought, I realized that I too had been part and parcel of this beautiful city and of that fast-moving motor traffic a decade ago!

Walking through downtown San Francisco I was amazed at the number of elderly men and women I met everywhere—in parks, stores, and restaurants. In my country we seldom come across elderly persons in such places. Especially in the principal thoroughfares, like the Ginza in Tokyo, we see among the crowd no one but young children and youthful men and women, who parade on the street as though rejoicing in their exuberant youthfulness. Japan is preponderantly a nation of youth. The birth of a million and a half babies each year maintains this disproportion of youngsters. On the other hand I was immediately impressed by the extraordinary longevity of Americans compared with a decade ago, when I had walked or motored about the United States. Are the advances in medicine and nutrition responsible? We Japanese age rather quickly because of severe living conditions, and for many reasons old people seldom have enough courage to come out in public and mingle freely with younger folks.

We had heard so much about the New York subways during the morning and evening rush hours: how the passengers were "jammed like sardines" into the trains. All members of my group took immense delight in riding the subways both in Chicago and New York. One evening at about 5:30 we happened to be in the heart of downtown Chicago and saw thousands of office workers making for Randolph Station. Apparently it was the same crowd of commuters that we see in Tokyo in the evening, eager to board the trains to get to their suburban homes, following their pigeon-like homing instinct. The prospective passengers came from all directions in the neighborhood, and the huge subway station seemed to be hardly able to absorb this ever-increasing crowd. I had fully expected that the trains would be filled to capacity and that I would be lucky if I could find a strap to hang onto in the car. What a surprise I had when I boarded the train and found that nearly everyone had a seat and that the train departed with only a few passengers standing.

New York subways were of course more crowded, but how comfortably I could travel even at the height of the rush hour, compared with what we were forced to go through in the Tokyo and Osaka subways. Our subway trains are so jammed that the proverbial American sardines applied to Japanese conditions is a decided understatement. You have to fight your way into a Japanese car. Waiting for the next train is no solution, as an even bigger crowd will be found both on the train and on the platform, and the situation becomes worse the longer you wait. Station crews on the platforms are often seen pushing people from behind into the car, just as the automatic electric door is about to close! Young children are often trampled down and many start

19

crying and groaning, but no one can possibly pay any attention. Passengers tread on your toes. Your shoes are often ruined. All are jostled about. Breathing is hard in the jammed car, so permeated with indescribably foul, warm air. It is an infernal sight. As a matter of fact, the Japanese refer to this state of affairs as *kotsu-jigoku,* or "transportation hell." Though the situation has greatly improved since the end of the war, such extreme congestion still occurs during the rush hours, especially with the rapid increase in urban population.

The average Japanese seems to be under the impression that all Americans go about very fashionably dressed. In the postwar craze to copy everything American, our people go to great lengths to imitate American styles and dress and do so rather ostentatiously. We were therefore quite bewildered to find that both American men and women were not particularly fussy about their clothes and that they were rather modestly dressed. How this contrasts with the Japanese situation, where many of us even go broke in our eagerness to be fashionably dressed; our vanity seems to know no bounds in this respect!

In the matter of eating, too, the average American is more sensible and budget-conscious. Many Japanese visitors to the United States since the war, despite the thinness of their pocketbooks, wish to dine at the very best restaurants. Not knowing Duncan Hines, they merely go to the most expensive hotels in the hope of getting an epicurean meal.

20

They were in many cases frankly disappointed. Ubiquitous self-service cafeterias are a unique American institution. One member of my group wondered if a similar cafeteria system introduced into Japan might not be a success. I expressed my opinion against such a venture. In a country like ours, where labor is cheap and plentiful, the people would rather be waited on in restaurants than stand in a "chow line." Moreover, the standard of living being so much lower in Japan makes it impossible for us to prepare or display as many dishes to choose from as are shown in American cafeterias. In point of fact, no one in my country, in spite of the widespread craze for things American, has to date introduced an American-style cafeteria, let alone an automat. However, we do have laundromats, though not many.

Although gone only half as long as the great New Yorker, I was a real Rip van Winkle in the sense that in coming from war-ravaged and impoverished Japan, coupled with a decade's absence, I rediscovered America—so gigantic, so prosperous, and so dynamic! It was this contrast which struck me more than anything else. Everything in this earthly world is relative, however. I remembered that five years before, when I returned to Japan from Soviet Russia, I was agreeably astonished to find Tokyo so very modern compared with Moscow, though Tokyo was a badly-battered city then. As I gradually readjusted myself to the new environment of America, I came to the conclusion that America had not changed very much during the last ten years,

21

as far as its physical aspect was concerned. New York was pretty much the same as when I last saw it nearly ten years before. I could not see any salient changes other than that Sixth Avenue had been re-named the Avenue of the Americas; that a TV station had been installed on the tower of the Empire State Building; and that the U.N. Headquarters building had been completed on the East River embankment, where it rises imposingly.

Washington, D.C. may have changed perhaps a little more. I noticed that almost every section, except the N.W., is now being inhabited by colored people. As for automobile congestion, one cannot park his car anywhere on any street without the risk of getting a ticket! Changes such as these, however, are not necessarily confined to the capital city, for we observed them elsewhere. Except for the phenomenal growth of suburban housing areas in many cities we visited, there is no building change throughout the United States comparable to that tak-ing place in my country, for the reconstruction of bombed-out cities of ashes and rubble has to be lived through to be believed.

On the other hand, I observed the tremendous social changes which have taken place among the American people during the last decade. I noticed a profound change in their outlook on life and even in their philosophy. Isolationism is definitely a thing of the past, even in the remote midwestern states. Americans are thinking of the defense of their land in terms of Berlin and Korea. They are keenly alive

22

to their responsibilities as the leaders of the Western democracies.

Millions of Americans must have visited Europe and Asia both during the war and in postwar years, either on tours of duty as servicemen or in other capacities. This visiting is a very significant fact. I noticed in most bookstores throughout the country "self-teaching" books on French, Spanish, or German, and even Russian and Asiatic languages, prominently displayed for sale. Such an array was not in evidence in prewar days, as far as I can remember. Americans today are more tolerant and more understanding of the problems of other peoples of the world. As for my own country, I reckon that no fewer than half a million Americans have either visited or stayed in the country since the end of the war. Members of my mission were often agreeably surprised at being "accosted" in Japanese by strangers in remote country places. They were friendly, hospitable, and helpful people and explained that they had been on Occupation duty in Japan. I began to think it was not safe to swear in my own language anywhere in the States!

A certain famous French writer once said that "we cannot hate the man whom we know." I believe there is much truth in that statement. I have in the past twenty years resided in many different countries of the world. Once I was assigned, against my wishes, to a country for which I had no particular liking. Perhaps I had a prejudice against the people and did not enjoy my sojourn in that

23

country. However, after I left, and the years rolled by, the unpleasant impressions I had gradually faded. I now have only fond memories of that country and its people. This philosophizing is perhaps human nature. This type of reaction is the same, I should venture to say, with many Americans in regard to my country.

To know the people and to study their idiosyncracies is the first step to the understanding of a nation. If, prior to World War II, half a million Americans had visited Japan, and if even one-tenth of that number of my countrymen could have paid a visit to the United States, I am firmly convinced that there would never have been a "Pearl Harbor." However, there are no doubt many foreigners who will never have the opportunity to visit my country and associate extensively with the Japanese, and others who, though honoring us with their presence, nevertheless may find themselves perplexed by many apparently incomprehensible aspects of Japanese living. It is my sincere hope that both groups will derive some benefit from the following chapters, in which I have tried to shed some light on the less well-known facts about my country's people and their customs.

2   Paper Houses, Bathhouses, and Teahouses

TO say, "Japanese houses are made of wood and paper," and let the statement stand, perpetuates a widespread misconception. They are certainly more than that! It is true that most Japanese houses look extremely flimsy to Westerners, especially those small houses which were built by the thousands in the bombed-out urban areas after the war. They are mostly of wooden construction, since timber is used extensively because of its easy availability. But our houses have beams and walls just like wooden houses in other parts of the world. Also, most windows and even sliding doors have glass panes, not just paper and wood. In general, I would say that a middle- or upper-class dwelling in Japan is not much flimsier than a California bungalow.

Several years ago an enterprising American trader started importing prefabricated houses to Japan, thinking that such imports would fulfill a need in this war-ravaged country. Contrary to general expectations, this enterprise did not do at all well. One of the many reasons for the failure was that the standard parts prefabricated in the United States were not suitable for house-construction in Japan. Japanese houses require many extra supports in order to make them earthquake-proof, and this factor was not taken into consideration by the American manufacturer.

The roof of the average Japanese house is quite solid, with thick, well-baked, and often gracefully-curved tiles dovetailing into each other. I have not seen wooden houses in other parts of the world with roofs built in such elaborate and substantial fashion. The roof of a California-style bungalow would not withstand the violent typhoons which sweep our country from time to time. As a matter of fact, after the war the United States Army requisitioned a number of purely Japanese-style houses in many parts of the country and made good use of them as living quarters, with very little alteration.

In the construction of Japanese houses, much attention is paid to ventilation in order to protect against the extreme dampness and sultriness of summer—wide windows, walls of small area, easily-detachable paper partitions, and a floor elevated high off the ground. One unfortunate result of this construction is that it makes Japanese houses extremely cold in winter.

In Tokyo and throughout that half of the country which lies north of it, winter is quite severe and lasts for perhaps six months of the year, from November to April. This is true in spite of the fact that northern Japan lies at a latitude from 38 to 45 degrees north, almost the same as northern California in America, and extending as far south as Spain and Portugal in Europe. Being situated this far south with its shores washed by the warm Japan Current, Japan should be much warmer in winter than it actually is. The reason that the country is unduly cold in winter months is because of the bleak cold wind which blows from the Siberian wilderness; furthermore, these winds are exceedingly damp, making the cold much more penetrating. However, the sky is usually very clear in Japan in the winter, and the sun is quite warm; so much so that Japanese houses have long been constructed in such a way as to take in as much sunshine as possible. All farmhouses in the Kanto plain north of Tokyo, where it is extremely windy during the winter months, have a very tall hedge grown at the back, or north side, of the house, which completely shelters the house. Each house has a spacious veranda facing due south, so as to obtain a maximum of the sun's warmth. In fact the entire house serves as a sunroom, so that the occupants can dispense with any heating arrangement. This ingenious system applies in varying degrees to the construction of almost all our houses.

27

At night and on cloudy or snowy days when there is no warmth from the sun, the people usually seek the warmth of their *kotatsu,* a small, square charcoal stove placed on the floor and covered with a wire netting, over which is spread a thick cotton-padded quilt. Several people squat around it and put their legs underneath the quilt, by which means the meager heat generated by the charcoal brazier, or *hibachi,* keeps their feet and bodies sufficiently warm. In most houses the brazier is built a good foot or so below the matted floor, so that one can sit and stretch his legs toward the brazier without the discomfort that squatting on the floor entails.

Although the exterior of Japanese houses is quite picturesque, especially those in the countryside with thatched roofs, it is the interior of the house which is most striking to Western eyes. The interior of our houses, especially from the point of view of a foreigner seeing it for the first time, is quite bare. The rooms are almost entirely devoid of furniture, the only ornaments being the *kakemono,* or hanging picture or calligraphy scroll, and perhaps some sprays of flowers arranged in a vase in an alcove. Many Westerners look upon this simplicity as something of a virtue, embodying the refined taste of the Japanese. This simplicity is, in fact, a keynote of all things Japanese. The floor of a Japanese room is covered with thick straw mats, called *tatami.* They are immaculate and a delight to walk on. Doors and partitions are all sliding ones, primarily in order to save space. *Shoji,* or detachable partitions, are truly made of "paper and wood," and are strikingly beautiful. They consist of wooden frames with many symmetrical sections, covered with white paper of exquisite quality. Many Westerners are quite entranced with them. On my recent visit to the States I saw that some of my American friends were using *shoji* which they brought back from Japan in their living rooms as screens, with very pleasing effect. This novel idea, I found, was greatly admired by their neighbors.

A Japanese room is bare mainly because it has to be used not only as a living room but also as a dining room, and often, too, as a bedroom. At night a whole set of bedding is taken from a closet and spread out on the matted floor. In the morning the bedding is again tucked away in the closet. For eating, we take out a small table about a foot high, around which the members of the family squat without chairs. When the meal is over, this table is again placed in the corner. With the room thus bare, it can be used for other purposes. Visitors may be shown into the same room and offered the *zabuton,* or cushion, to sit upon. Thus a large number of people can live in a comparatively small house, making maximum use of all available space.

I once rented a two-storied Japanese-style residence of medium size in Tokyo. It was a house which normally could have housed five or six members of a Japanese family, living quite comfortably in Japanese fashion. However, I did not care to live in Japanese style, so I furnished the whole house in

29

Western style, by converting and arranging the rooms into living room, dining room, and bedroom. Then much to my surprise I found the house too small even for myself alone! The minimum number of pieces of Western-style furniture I brought in were crowding each other and took up so much space that the whole house looked like a second-hand furniture store.

As I have travelled about various parts of the globe, I have realized what little room the average Japanese needs in his daily living; and thus how eighty-eight million people have managed to live in a country not larger than the single state of California, and furthermore with only eighteen per cent of its total land area being arable. Simplicity, then, by necessity, is the keynote of our living.

My countrymen, if they could afford it, would prefer living in the more comfortable, Western-style houses. In the late 'twenties and all through the 'thirties, when the Japanese economy was on the upgrade, the fashion for a middle-class man was to build his house with a special foreign-style annex. The average house in those days, especially in urban areas, had this extra room, built entirely in the Western style, in which tables and chairs and other Western furniture were placed. This room was used mainly for receiving visitors, so they would not have to go through the ordeal of crossing their legs and squatting on the floor.

The Japanese habit of taking a communal bath is well known. For the sake of the uninitiated, however, a native bathhouse may be described as something like a miniature gymnasium within a wooden building. The bath establishment is divided into two sections, one for men and the other for women. The customer enters the building and takes off his *geta,* or wooden clogs, and pays a fee of ¥15, or about four cents, at the counter. Then, on a spacious wooden floor, he strips himself and puts his outer garments and underwear in a wicker basket provided to each individual by the bathhouse. He then walks into the bathroom proper, which is partitioned off from the dressing room by glass windows.

In the communal bathroom there is a rectangular wooden or tile tub about twelve feet long, ten feet wide, and three feet deep, which can accommodate from ten to twenty persons at one time. The tub is brimming with hot water, which is usually so exceptionally hot—over 110 degrees Fahrenheit in many cases—that no Westerner with fairer skin would be able to stand it. The prospective bather first washes his body thoroughly with hot water, provided in taps along the walls of the bathroom proper, before he steps into the tub, for he does not dare to pollute the water. My countrymen are most fond of a really hot bath; they immerse their bodies in the deep tub so long that they come out colored as red as lobsters! They then set to rubbing their entire bodies with soap and hand-towels or sponges, all the while helping themselves liberally to warm tap water provided from the outlets along the wall. The floor is spacious enough so that twenty to thirty people can easily squat on it to scrub their bodies and wash their hair. All these washings are carried on outside the tub.

The public bathhouse is most crowded in the evening when most people have finished their day's work; perhaps fifty to one hundred people may be taking a bath at the same time. I should say that while my countrymen display considerable shyness in exposing their bodies in public, in the bathhouse they shake off their diffidence entirely and turn the whole bathhouse into a kind of nudist club! I have said that the communal bathhouse is separated into two sections for segregation of the sexes. This segregation is complete with only one exception: in the bathhouse for a few extra yen one can hire a *sansuke,* a husky young man to scrub your back. Quite a few bathers ask for the service of this professional man, for he not only scrubs your body but also kneads the muscles of your neck and arms in the bargain. It is certainly pleasing to have one's body massaged by this youthful masseur. Unlike other bathers he appears for his duties with a type of swimming trunks on. Now this male *sansuke* also performs the same service for nude female bathers in the women's section. Strangely enough, there are no female *sansuke* in any part of the country.

The Japanese do not share the American's liking for a shower bath. They seldom used it before the Occupation, nor do they particularly like it now. Their idea of a bath is not confined to cleaning the body, for their conception goes beyond this basic

32

operation. They soak their bodies thoroughly in the deep bath and enjoy the pleasant feeling which overheating the entire body gives. To most of my countrymen a shower bath is unsatisfactory in that it does not provide the same enjoyment that is obtained by deep immersion in the tub. A friend of mine, a Japanese, after intensive house-hunting in San Francisco some years ago, finally found a very attractive house for rent. The bathroom, however, contained only a shower, so my friend gave up the house, a very desirable one in every other respect, simply for lack of a bathtub.

The communal bathhouse in Japan has been a time-honored institution for many centuries. On an average, one thousand people a day visit one bathhouse. It naturally serves as a meeting place for the people in the neighborhood. Since my countrymen bathe quite often—some almost every day—they meet their neighbors and friends in the public bath and exchange greetings and gossip. In the large tub in which perhaps more than a dozen persons are enjoying soaking themselves at the same time, some people take advantage of the opportunity to advertise certain stores, boost certain political candidates, or worse still, spread communist propaganda. All these touts feign a casual tone of voice, so that their remarks may be believed by the other bathers.

The Japanese passion for hot baths can be explained by economic and physical reasons. The Japanese house has no heating arrangement in winter, save perhaps for a meager charcoal fire in a small brazier, which is kept barely alive and just hot enough to boil the water of a tiny tea kettle. Most of my countrymen are so poor that they cannot afford even a modest coal or gas stove, let alone a central heating system. As a result, the Japanese may be said to be half-frozen in winter. American officials during the Occupation were often surprised to find Japanese hands icy cold, when they shook hands with visitors arriving in the well-heated American offices in winter time. It is true that some of our office buildings and trains are now moderately heated, but you may count upon our houses being invariably cold. Under such physical conditions, a hot bath naturally provides a very desirable internal heating system for us. By a stay in a really hot bath for quite some time, our bodies remain warm for many hours afterward in chilly rooms, even in ones completely devoid of heat.

A further reason for this communal bath institution is economic. There is a tremendous saving in water and fuel when a thousand people can use the same hot water in a comparatively small tub, instead of everyone taking an individual bath at home.

This discussion of Japanese public bathhouses reminds me of a visit I made to a Soviet bathhouse when I was in Moscow several years ago. I was on the embassy staff there during the war years. I was very curious about many things the Russians did, for example, their not using paper at all after relieving themselves! I found that most Russians, like my countrymen, frequented a public-bath establishment, which was government-owned. My curiosity was aroused and I decided one day to visit a near-by bathhouse, defying the vigilant eyes of the secret police agents who always trailed me, sometimes secretively and at other times straightforwardly. After standing in a long queue, I entered the bathhouse, and upon payment of a few rubles at the counter, I was given a tiny cake of soap, which was about the same size as the free cake of soap given in American hotels. The interior of the bathhouse, both the anteroom in which you undress and the bathroom itself, bore striking resemblances to Japanese public baths. The bathroom, however, was devoid of a tub; instead, the whole bathroom was filled with warm steam vapor. There were the familiar rows of hot and cold water taps along the wall, as in a Japanese public bath. However, the total effect was like that of a Turkish bath. The way the Russians scrubbed their bodies squatting on the tiled floor was pretty much the same as in Japan. Both the Russian and the Japanese people are extremely poor, judged by American standards, and in order to economize both in fuel and water, they too must fall back on the public-bath arrangement.

Another reason for using such hot water for bathing is medical. The Japanese consume a great deal of salt in the form of *shoyu,* a soybean sauce, salted fish, and pickles. In fact, one of the characteristics of our cuisine is its almost complete lack of sweets. We are inveterate drinkers of unsweetened green tea—at home, in offices, and on trains. Most offices employ young girls whose only task is to make and serve tea to the office staff and to customers and visitors. Now this almost continuous tea-drinking habit is born of necessity. We have to drink copious amounts of tea in order to counteract the effects of the excessive salt we eat. I myself try to subsist on Western food, having been used to it for so long and not being particularly partial to *shoyu* or rice. However, once in a while I have to eat a complete Japanese meal, and then I become very thirsty and keep on drinking water for hours afterward. Many of my countrymen complain about American food being too sweet. I knew one Japanese admiral in prewar years who, while journeying on the American continent, always carried with him a bottle of soybean sauce and sprinkled it on whatever food was served to him in restaurants. Hot baths with their attendant perspiration serve as a natural antidote against too much salt in the body.

Oddly enough, my countrymen take equally hot baths in summer, for then the weather is not only very hot but also extremely sultry. A hot bath is thought to produce a reaction of cooling immediately after the bath. So there is a national indulgence in boiling hot baths all year round.

Not all Japanese go to a communal bath. The well-to-do have their own bathrooms in their homes. Here the bath is usually a wooden affair, but in some homes it is constructed of marble or tile. Members of a family immerse themselves in the same hot water in the tub, but they soap and scrub their bodies outside the tub, just as do the patrons of the public bath.

Hotspring baths are found almost everywhere in my country. There are actually more than 1,100 mineral baths, of which 656 are thermal springs. The temperature of these hotsprings ranges anywhere from 80 degrees Fahrenheit to 226 degrees. The hottest water used for bathing is that at Kusatsu, a small town one hundred and twenty miles north of Tokyo, where baths are taken at one hundred and twenty degrees, an almost unbelievable temperature for a bath.

Hotspring baths are truly delightful, provided the temperature is not too hot. At many resort hotels, baths are built in a very elaborate fashion, usually with marble, stone, or fancy-colored tile. In these hotels abundant water from the hotsprings is conducted into the great bathroom, in which the big pool is very much like an indoor swimming pool. At the Fujiya, the internationally-renowned hotel in the mountain resort of Hakone, some seventy miles west of Tokyo, there are two strikingly splendid baths, named the Aquarium and the Mermaids. The former has glass walls and is surrounded by an aquarium, while the latter is decorated with fantastically-carved mermaid statues. Immersing oneself in the hotspring pool, which is welling up all the time, and gazing at the fancy goldfish dancing up and down in the floodlit aquarium, one forgets all his worldly cares

37

and finds himself in a state of ecstacy. This is bathing at its best, and one can even imagine that he is bathing in one of those fabulous Roman baths in which many an emperor bathed during the heyday of the great Roman Empire.

Thousands of GI's, officers, and their families who have come to Japan since the end of the war have experienced our hotspring baths. Most of them seem to have enjoyed them very much.

In no other country in the world do the four seasons alternate with such clock-like regularity. It is a surprising fact, considering that Japan, though a tiny country composed of a chain of islands, extends for some 1,500 miles from north to south. European and other countries are subject to a very changeable climate. In the British Isles, whose geographical position is somewhat analogous to Japan, inhabitants often shiver in June and sweat in a December heat wave. Such atmospheric phenomena are utterly unknown in Japan. Punctuality of the four seasons is such that, throughout the country, people stop bathing in the sea abruptly at the end of August and begin again in the middle of July. Likewise, our worst storms seem to come on certain days each year.

Our popular pastimes, apart from baseball and other imported sports, invariably have something to do with nature, for which the great regularity of the seasons is in part responsible. In spring, cherry blossoms bloom early in April. There are many cherry groves, similar in size to the one on the Potomac River in Washington, D.C., to which many people in groups, both large and small, go on picnics. Under the gorgeous cherry blossoms, holiday crowds revel in drinking and other forms of merrymaking. In autumn, when the leaves of trees change color, maple-leaf viewing is the occasion for nation-wide outings. Among the various trees, the Japanese maple is by far the most striking and variegated in color. Here and there in the mountains there are maple groves to which the people flock to admire the autumn brilliance, when the leaves are at their most beautiful. Even bleak winter is not without its quota of nature-loving pastimes. Older people, especially, take delight in admiring snow scenery, when gardens and mountains are wrapped in this white garb. Gazing at the snow scenery from a veranda of a house or inn and sipping heated saké, a native rice wine, out of a tiny cup, has always been a favorite pastime. This type of enjoyment has always been considered highly esthetic by my countrymen. It is customary on such occasions for the participants in the gathering to compose poems. Here there is a joviality and a conviviality with a deeply satisfying inner feeling which gives us lasting pleasure. This type of pastime should have a universal appeal, for is it not friendship at its best?

Flowers, mountains and rivers, mist and rain have been the principal themes of our drawings from ancient times. Thus, early Japanese drawings and paintings were usually devoid of animals or human beings. This innate love of nature in the Japanese people has given rise to such time-honored

39

customs as the tea ceremony, flower arrangement, moon-viewing festival, and the like.

As a result of this inborn love of nature, along with the fact that the Japanese have for centuries been confirmed vegetarians, due to the extensive influence of Buddhism, we are as a general rule not given to brutality. I have known many of my countrymen whose hearts grew faint while visiting the famous Chicago stockyards, and who could not eat meat for several days afterwards.

The Japanese, mainly because of overcrowding and the scarcity of natural resources, have been accustomed to perennial poverty from ancient times and have contrived various methods to compensate for it. Their efforts, however, have not been directed towards conquering nature, but rather in the negative way of making the best of what nature has to offer. They have tried to adapt themselves to nature, rather than to control or subjugate it. I have often questioned whether man can really control or subjugate nature.

Our people have never seriously attempted to utilize the abundant supply of hotspring water in order to provide heat for buildings and homes, even in a small commercial way. Years ago when I visited Iceland, I saw in the outskirts of Reykjavik a greenhouse in which tomatoes were being grown by using the water of a hotspring. Such an idea could be adopted to advantage in Japan, where thermal springs are found almost everywhere. I have told many people here about it, but apparently they are too conservative to utilize this wonderful source of heat. Instead, my countrymen seem to be content with sunshine and a tiny charcoal fire and depend solely on these for heating purposes.

Living like hermits for centuries in the narrow confines of their miniature land, my countrymen have learned to live in utmost simplicity and frugality, and to seek pleasure and contentment in that which nature freely provides.

3 The Japanese Woman in Kimono

THERE is a popular saying in my country that living in an American-style house with a Japanese wife and eating Chinese food constitutes an ideal living arrangement. An American home, with its labor-saving devices and efficient plumbing and heating, is no doubt the best dwelling in the world and the envy, I believe, of many less fortunate peoples, including the Japanese.

The Japanese are particularly impressed by the modern American kitchen with its refrigerator, electric stove, and sink with garbage disposer. No doubt they should be impressed, for a Japanese kitchen is usually very gloomy. It has practically no modern conveniences, save perhaps a gas burner, and the sink is usually an affair of tin and wood.

One of the members of our inspection group to the United States recently held a very high government position. He lived a reasonably comfortable life at home. When he visited an American home and was shown the kitchen, he remarked that he was glad his wife did not accompany him to America. She would have held up her hands in despair and refused to work in her own kitchen, once she had seen an American one.

In spite of the material superiority of American kitchens, it is the Chinese cuisine which is world famous for its variety and for those of its dishes which enjoy universal gastronomic appeal. Though French cooking may be considered more palatable to the Occidental, there is no doubt that the Chinese are excellent cooks who can concoct many delectable dishes.

On the other hand, it is the Japanese wife who is most faithful and devoted to her husband and to the household, even to the point of servility. The Japanese wife considers that her mission is to bear and rear children, and to perpetuate the tradition of the family into which she has wed.

Living in an antiquated house with no modern conveniences worthy of the name, the Japanese wife usually spends most of her time drudging away in her house. Even with domestic help, the Japanese wife in a middle- or upper-class home is confined to the house almost all day, and it is rare that her husband takes her out to dinner or to a show.

The Japanese husband seeks his own pleasure in his own way—in a geisha house or at a restaurant. The Japanese seldom entertain at home, for to do so has long been considered a lack of respectability. Only a mean or poor person is said to resort to such informal entertaining. Parties, if they have to be given at all, must be given in a restaurant or a tea-house, and since Japanese parties are essentially men's affairs, usually waited upon by geisha host-esses, the Japanese wife has practically no chance of attending such functions and so has to stay at home most of the time.

Concubinage is an institution still somewhat prevalent in my country, although not half as widespread as in China. I am told that the institution of mistresses can still be found in the Americas and in Europe. Originally the concubine system of Asia grew out of the Oriental custom of having to per-petuate family tradition through the male lineage. Therefore, if a wife failed to give birth to a son, the husband was permitted to keep a concubine or two in order to secure a son. The average husband today, however, finds it difficult to provide only for his wife and children. So the system here is rapidly disappearing.

Therefore, to keep a concubine is looked upon as a sign of prosperity. The system in Japan is a product of our family life in which the wife, to all intents and purposes, occupies a position of servant or even virtual slave. The Japanese male, moreover, has no opportunity to meet women socially, such as at cocktail or dinner parties. The parties they attend are, almost without exception, stag affairs, waited upon by professional hostesses. Besides, divorce is a thing not lightly resorted to in my country, as we are very critical of divorces, and to be divorced usually lowers one's prestige and reputation in the eyes of others. Such being the case, once married to a woman, a man has to continue with her, irrespective of what happens, even if there is little love or affection between them. As he becomes more wealthy, the Japanese man has more occasion to frequent teahouses and restaurants. If he is a businessman or a politician, a great deal of business is transacted at such places. Geisha hostesses at the teahouses are usually beautiful, more beautiful than his wife, who ages rather quickly because of domestic drudgery and frequent childbirth. Geisha compete with each other to obtain a patron, so as to secure for themselves a means of living when they grow old. The rich client, on his part, tries to keep one favorite girl in order to put up a show of prosperity, with its consequent enhancement of his social prestige.

I know one business executive who is opposed to the very idea of concubinage and who therefore has never shown any liking for these professional girls. He once told me in confidence that he was distinctly at a handicap in his business dealings, for his prestige suffered a great deal on account of his not keeping a concubine!

Concubinage is naturally a source of serious

family disputes, but the Japanese wife usually has to submit finally to this intolerable situation. She usually makes up for her misery and unhappiness in the loving care of her children.

Although since the war our young women have come to mix more freely with young men, they are still backward in their ideas and manners, and do not know how to behave properly in a mixed gathering. In Shanghai, where there was a large Japanese colony before the war, American or European consuls used to hold large receptions. Many leading officials and businessmen of my country were invited to these functions with their wives. The Japanese guests, after passing the reception line, lost no time in separating according to sex: the men left their wives and engaged in conversation and drinking with other men; the wives themselves congregated in a group. Thus there was complete segregation until the time came for the couples to leave.

Japanese women usually make good wives when they marry Westerners. On the other hand marriages between Japanese men and foreign girls have often proved to be failures. Nowhere is Kipling's adage that "East is East and West is West" truer than in the case of a Japanese man's marriage to an Occidental woman, for Japanese men have not learned chivalry in the Western sense of the word. This shortcoming results in an attitude toward women often unnatural and uncouth. Moreover, Japanese men, however Westernized in their youth, become more Japanese as they grow older and tend

47

to revert more and more to typical Japanese ways.

A rather prominent Japanese businessman, when he was in the London office of his firm, married an English girl, and the couple lived a happy married life for more than twenty years in various parts of Europe and America. They reared two lovely Eurasian children and were a popular couple wherever they went. His firm, a business company of international renown, paid him liberally, so he and his family lived a life of comparative luxury. When the Pacific War broke out, the couple were repatriated to Japan, this being the English wife's first visit to her husband's country. Things started to go wrong with the couple as soon as they arrived in Japan. The wife, who was used to a good living and was somewhat spoiled, found the wartime austerity and privation in Japan too much to bear. When near the end of the war a large-scale American bombing set fire to the city in which they lived, the husband quit the house in a hurry to seek refuge, leaving his wife and children in the house, which was in serious danger. The British wife was so disgusted by this act and others that she finally made up her mind to leave her husband once and for all and as soon as transportation was available went back to England with her children.

The late Dr. Nitobe, an internationally-famed publicist, who worked for years in the secretariat of the now defunct League of Nations in Geneva, had an American wife. Theirs was generally conceded to be one of the most successful East-West marriages. In spite of this, Dr. Nitobe in his late years was said to have been miserable as far as his meals were concerned. He was starving for *chazuke*, a Japanese meal consisting of hot tea poured over boiled rice and eaten with pickles. His wife, however, insisted on Western food, and there were disagreements. Many a time Dr. Nitobe used to slip into the kitchen in the middle of the night and prepare the Japanese meal himself.

While such cases of unfortunate East and West marriages have been all too numerous, Japanese women who have married Westerners generally make exemplary wives.

In the early Meiji era, that is, around the 'nineties of the last century, not long after Japan was opened for foreign intercourse, the Austro-Hungarian Empire maintained a legation in Tokyo. Count Coudenhove was stationed in Tokyo as military attaché to the legation. This youthful Austrian, who came from a very distinguished family, used to go horseback riding every morning. While riding one day this nobleman met and fell in love with a Japanese woman, by the name of Mitsuko, whom he eventually married. Upon their return to Austria the Coudenhoves led a very happy life, and Countess Coudenhove, despite many handicaps, was duly accepted in Viennese high society, which in the days of the Austro-Hungarian Empire was exceedingly glamorous. Dainty little Mitsuko was not only a popular social figure in Vienna, but true to her Japanese tradition, a good wife who bore and reared eight children. The Coudenhove children were brought up in the Japanese tradition of filial piety and paternalism, and they all became useful citizens of the empire. The eldest son, Richard Coudenhove-Kalergi, was the author of a celebrated book on Pan-Europe, and he, together with Aristide Briand, long-time foreign minister of France, was largely instrumental in the creation of the League of Nations after the first World War.

I knew another son of Count and Countess Coudenhove who was adviser to the Japanese Legation in Prague, Czechoslovakia, where I served in pre-war years. This Mr. Coudenhove was an exceedingly affable man and a popular figure in diplomatic circles in Prague. He did much to interpret Japan to European peoples, and I remember his paying frequent visits to his mother, Countess Coudenhove, who had already reached an advanced age and was living in seclusion in a castle near Vienna. The Coudenhove children were the embodiment of all that is best in the Japanese tradition of family life.

Mention must also be made of Lady Arnold of London. Her deceased husband was an eminent British educator, who was knighted by the king many years ago. Lady Arnold is a Japanese woman of considerable charm and intelligence and has been a popular figure in London social circles. She has done much to further the cause of Anglo-Japanese friendship and has lived up to the best traditions of Japanese womanhood.

Another Japanese woman of international fame

is Oyuki Morgan, a Kyoto-born girl who married George D. Morgan, a nephew of J. P. Morgan of the fabulous Morgan family. She lived in pomp and luxury and in her later years resided in Nice on the French Riviera. Some years ago, Oyuki, then a widow, was so homesick that she decided to come back to her native Kyoto to live in retirement. When she returned to her native country, however, she was besieged day and night by numerous people, from canvassers who tried to sell her life insurance policies to those unscrupulous people who attempted to extort money by various dishonest means, knowing that she still enjoyed a chunk of the fabulous Morgan fortune. Realizing that everyone had an eye on her fortune, Oyuki was visibly annoyed and did not find her seclusion in Kyoto at all secure. She has kept to herself and is not at home to anyone except the priest of the Xavier Church to which she belongs. Oyuki still lives in Kyoto, shunning all publicity.

Dr. Hideki Yukawa, who lectured for some years at Columbia University and who was awarded the much-coveted Nobel Prize for his studies in atomic theory a few years ago, is one of the few people postwar Japan can be proud of. He is the only physicist who has been able to explain the forces that hold the earth together. When he came back to Japan recently, Dr. Yukawa was given a big welcome, but at the same time was said to have been annoyed by experiences similar to Oyuki Morgan's. The Japanese are poor and therefore restless. They are very inquisitive and like to pry into other people's affairs. It is hard to make a living, and if anyone is known to be wealthy or famous, they resort to all conceivable means to exploit his reputation or extort his riches.

The Japanese woman is exceedingly patient. She has to put up with all kinds of hardship and to bear even her husband's unkind acts, such as his keeping a concubine. By Japanese custom, she is wedded into her husband's *family,* not just to the husband himself, and once in the family it is her duty and mission to uphold the tradition of the family. Therefore, divorce is unthinkable and is considered something dishonorable, even if all the wrongs are on the side of the husband. If, however, the situation becomes utterly intolerable and she really wants a divorce, she usually finds herself with half a dozen children. For the sake of the childen she is often dissuaded from taking such a drastic step. Also, she would be unable to support herself. Thus, poverty and too many children make her subservient to her husband, however tyrannical he may be.

In the Japanese home the husband is omnipotent. Middle- and upper-class families usually have a private bath in their house. The bath is a usual Japanese one, with hot water kept in the tub for soaking and warming one's body and not changed more than once a day. The privilege of taking the first bath is invariably accorded to the master of the house, and after him come the children, then his wife, and finally the servants of the household.

At dinner the husband usually gets an extra dish of the best delicacy. For instance, raw fish is considered a very dainty food in my country, but it is rather expensive. In most households, even when there is not enough raw fish to go around, the husband either monopolizes the dish or gets the largest helping of it. It is thought in Japan that the husband is the mainstay of the family, and since the entire family subsists by his earnings anyway, due respect should be paid to him and he should be fed better than other members of the family.

The fortitude and self-denial with which the Japanese woman tolerates all kinds of discomfort and difficulties have become second nature. Japanese women giving birth in an American or European maternity hospital have often been the subject of considerable admiration on the part of hospital nurses and doctors. I remember once visiting a London hospital in which a Japanese friend of my wife's was giving birth. Quite a few Japanese residents used to send their wives to this particular hospital for childbirth. A doctor there told me that he had never heard any Japanese lady cry in the throes of delivery, while all the British patients groaned fiercely and in some cases even swore. The doctor said that he sometimes even wondered if Japanese women felt pain at all during delivery! The Japanese woman thinks it extremely disgraceful to howl and groan in such cases and would try to suppress all her agonies with the fortitude and patience characteristic of the women of her race.

For a variety of reasons, the Japanese wife's housekeeping is extremely onerous. For one thing, her kitchen is so primitive that she has to spend hours on end preparing meals. Except in major urban areas, gas is not generally used for cooking. She has to get up early in the morning to make a charcoal fire in the brazier. Rice has to be washed and cooked for each meal, for the family-members like to eat rice hot, even when other dishes may be served cold. Moreover, washing dishes afterward is a tedious process, so many more bowls and plates being used than in Western cooking. Each vegetable, and even the pickles, have to be served in separate bowls and plates. The wife cannot enlist the help of her husband in dish-washing as in American homes. The Japanese husband thinks it beneath his dignity to condescend to work in the kitchen and leaves everything to his wife, even when domestic help is not available. The average Japanese wife spends at least two hours in preparing breakfast alone.

The Japanese way of making the bed at night and tucking the bedding away into the closet again in the morning calls for considerably more time and labor than making the bed in Western homes.

The Japanese house has to be dusted and cleaned thoroughly every day, for it is very dusty in most cities, since most streets and sidewalks are either not paved at all or are imperfectly paved. The house is usually wide open and has many cracks, so that sweeping the house is a task which requires the constant attention and vigilance of the housewife.

The Japanese, both men and women, generally dress in native kimono at home, although they wear foreign dress while at work. This dual living adds another headache to the Japanese housewife, for a kimono has to be tailored at home by the women. Thus, the Japanese wife lives in a dreary routine of housekeeping day in and day out, and if she has children, her work is made doubly onerous.

Loyalty of the Japanese wife to her husband is a virtue excelled in by few other peoples, I believe. To counteract the stress which modern conditions have imposed on this institution of loyalty, we Japanese have a story which we like to repeat to our families. This story of the wife of Kazutoyo Yamanouchi, a feudal warrior, is proverbial:

Yamanouchi was a low-ranking warrior in the service of Lord Nobunaga Oda, a celebrated feudal chieftain in the sixteenth century. One day a horse dealer came from a northern province with a splendid mount. Yamanouchi, being ambitious, was very tempted to buy the horse, as the possession of a good steed was a sure step to promotion among the warrior class of those days. However, he could not afford it. He appeared so despondent that his wife insisted on knowing the nature of his worry. Though in feudal days a warrior considered it shameful and beneath his dignity to consult his wife on any matter pertaining to his duties, Yamanouchi confided in his wife. Upon hearing the story, she produced ten pieces of gold, which she had long kept stored in secret in the drawer of her mirror stand. Yamanouchi was surprised to find his wife with so much money, but she explained that it was her dowry and that her mother had enjoined her not to spend it except in the case of urgent need by her husband. Even though the couple were poverty-stricken for a long time, she had never thought of using this money, for her mother's words always rang in her ears and restrained her. Now she was glad she had not waited in vain! Yamanouchi bought the fine horse with the money, and his lord was very pleased with him. From then on Yamanouchi distinguished himself in the domain and was finally made a local baron.

We have always liked this story as an illustration of our ancestral virtues. In modern times, too, we have striking and dramatic accounts of the loyalty of Japanese wives.

In February, 1936 a number of disgruntled young officers of the Japanese Army, with some of their loyal enlisted men, staged a large-scale insurrection in Tokyo. They seized the principal government offices and assassinated a host of prominent statesmen known to be opposed to the radical expansionist policy of the military. The twenty-sixth of February, 1936 has gone down in the Japanese history as a dreadful day.

A group of these rebels took machine guns and other weapons from their garrison and broke into the home of Viscount Saito, former Prime Minister, to kill him. For a few terrible moments, Viscountess Saito placed herself in front of her husband and said to the brigands: "Kill me instead—my husband cannot be spared by the country." She actually put her hand on the mouth of the roaring machine gun until her wounds forced her aside. Several other bloodthirsty rebels forced their way into the house of General Watanabe, Inspector General of Military Education. In the frightful tragedy there, Mrs. Watanabe lay down with her husband in her arms, so that the assassins had to force the gun underneath her body to complete their dastardly act.

Japanese history is full of examples of such heroism and loyalty of woman to their husbands.

The Japanese women's lot, however unenviable, cannot be branded as altogether miserable. There is one redeeming feature at least. When she becomes old and her children are all grown and earning their own living, the elderly mother is usually well taken care of by them, and also by her grandchildren. Most mothers live under the same roof with their children, who consider it their duty to see that their father and mother are properly looked after in their old age. It is then that the Japanese mother can look back over her years of almost incessant toil and know that her self-sacrifice has not been in vain.

I have seen many American widows far along in years living in hotels alone. I suppose that in most such cases they are left with a certain amount of money, either from old age insurance or in some form of savings. However, we in Japan would believe that as such women grow older they would inevitably become lonesome, restless, and even hysterical.

Their unhappiness would be further aggravated by the need to be careful in spending money. Since the keynote of Western society is individualism, such situations as this are no doubt taken for granted. To me, however, a Japanese widow looks infinitely happier, surrounded by her children and grand-children. She is usually beaming with contentment and happiness, secure in the knowledge that none of her offspring will desert her, even until the very day she breathes her last.

Six years of Allied Occupation had a salutary effect on the relationship between the sexes in Japan. I believe that millions are grateful for the change. Coeducation has been encouraged, and young women are mixing more freely and naturally with men. More and more young men are finding their wives among their own circle of girl friends, and such mar-riages, as far as can be judged thus far, have been largely successful. No longer are a couple walking arm in arm down the street frowned upon, nor does their act evoke the curious stares and disapproving grimaces of passers-by, as in prewar years.

Women's suffrage was finally put into practice after the war. Women before took little interest in their own government; in some cases, none at all. When women voted in the general election for the first time in 1946, there was a certain misunder-standing: many voters, particularly in rural areas, had the mistaken idea that women had to vote for women candidates and that men voted for men. Such laughable misconceptions, however, no longer exist, and the turn-out of women voters in recent elections has been as good as that of men.

There has been a marked increase in the number of women working in governmental offices and in the professions, in competition with men. This is a result mainly of the economic difficulties experienced by many households in postwar years. However, there is a definite and encouraging sign that women are demanding and obtaining equal rights with men. It now appears that emancipation of women is well on the way to achievement.

Such an observation, however, cannot but be a superficial one. In the turmoil and social upheaval of postwar years relationships between men and women have become extremely lax. It is well known to us that the Japanese as a race are prone to go from one extreme to the other. Many young men and women today are blindly imitating Western habits and customs, and deprecate everything Japanese. However, many millions of my countrymen, especially in rural areas, are still strongly conservative. Their primitive agricultural methods have not altered very much; for changes come slowly. Women continue to rear large families with little thought of their future economic status or prospects. Likewise, in urban areas, there has been little effort made to "modernize the home," and women today—even in large cities—still have to work like slaves in their own households. Similarly, during their youth, men may go out freely with girl friends or with their wives, but as they grow older they will revert to

59

the old customs and follow in their fathers' footsteps. Though perhaps not to the same extent as their fathers, they will still continue to seek enjoyment largely outside their homes, which means that their wives will go on toiling in the household.

The pendulum for behavior in Japan today has swung very widely to the radical side, but it is bound to swing back. Undoubtedly, the emancipation of women from feudalistic ideas and customs will have to await a general awakening among the women of Japan to their human rights. Furthermore, in order for such emancipation to be permanent, there will have to be created an environment that will enable women to function as the social and intellectual equals of men. As long as women continue to bear and rear half a dozen children, and our standard of living remains as low as it is now, not much hope can be entertained for a real emancipation of Japanese womanhood.

More and more women and girls in my country have of late adopted Western-style dress. In fact, one of the most lucrative professions in postwar years has been ladies' dressmaking. It is indeed the fashion now for Japanese girls to be dressed in Western garb. This is a fad, however, and has been exaggerated by the fact that most Japanese lost their kimonos during the war in the long, terrible bombings and fires.

Nevertheless, the kimono is coming back into its own. Semi-rural and rural women still wear the kimono. Geisha in teahouses, even though generally young, have not discarded their native costume. It is remarkable what different pictures a Japanese woman presents in kimono and in Western dress. No doubt, the kimono is a graceful garment for the Japanese, for it conceals their typically short legs. But it is a most uncomfortable garment to wear, since the *obi,* or broad sash, stifles one's chest. The kimono completely deprives one of freedom of movement. Though Western dress does not become those Japanese women with especially short legs, it does at least give them freedom of movement, and it even gives some women a rather aggressive look. We Japanese men are hard judges at times!

The Japanese woman dressed in kimono is a symbol to us of traditional womanhood, embodying those virtues of self-sacrifice, devotion, and patience on behalf of the husband and the family. The increasing number of women dressed in Western clothes symbolizes the general aspiration of Japanese women to become the social and intellectual equals of men. No doubt a happy medium will eventually be reached and a Japanese womanhood evolved which will combine the best elements of both Japanese and Western traditions.

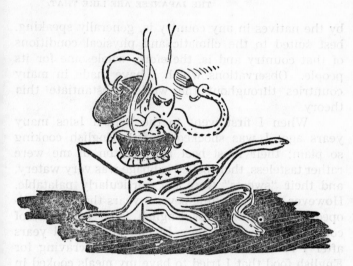

4   Boiled Octopus and Broiled Eels

JAPANESE food, however unsubstantial and weird it may seem to the Occidental, with its raw fish, eels, octopuses, and heaps of rice, is the end-product of many centuries of experimentation by the inhabitants of Japan. To evaluate any country's foods and dishes one must carefully consider the available materials, climatic conditions, and physical requirements of the native people. Food consumed by the natives in any country is, generally speaking, best suited to the climatic and physical conditions of that country and is, therefore, wholesome for its people. Observations which I have made in many countries throughout the world substantiate this theory.

When I first went to the British Isles many years ago, I was shocked to find English cooking so plain; their roast beef and mutton to me were rather tasteless, their boiled cabbage was very watery, and their "sweets" were not particularly palatable. However, after spending several years there, I developed a great liking for English food, which is, of course, very wholesome. In fact, for several years after I returned to Japan I had such a craving for English food that I tried to have my meals cooked in the plain English way and even sent for an English cookbook. Particularly did I miss English tea. I learned while in England and Scotland how to make tea in the orthodox way and thought that I would thereafter be able to have English tea wherever I went. But in Japan and elsewhere, however hard you may try to make tea in the correct English fashion, the resulting beverage is never really the same, even if you use the rather expensive Lipton tea. I suppose that tea tastes so good in England mainly because of the water there, and because of that peculiar British humidity.

Similarly, when I went to Soviet Russia I learned quickly that Russian food is best suited for that rigorous climate and that it is by far the most

wholesome food one can eat in that country. During
my first year in Soviet Russia I found vodka, the
favorite Russian drink, most abominable. It was
too explosive for me, and I would not touch it. It
was not only very strong but also tasteless; I thought
I would rather drink gasoline. However, as I continued to live in that country, I began to like vodka.
At the end of my fourth year in Russia, I found
nothing quite as good as a glass of vodka on a cold
wintery evening, taken with *zakuski,* a rich Russian
canapé. My foreign friends of other embassies had
similar experiences.

After many years' residence abroad, I have
come to the conclusion that the best way to keep fit
in any country is to eat and live like a native. Incidentally, this mode of living is by far the cheapest.
In China, the Chinese do not eat cold food except
perhaps "rotten eggs" and a few other special items.
They never drink cold tea or water. If you travel
in the back country, you will see even the poorest
coolies at a roadside stall eating piping hot meals
and drinking boiling hot tea. Now it is a well-known
fact that sanitary conditions in China, especially with
regard to foodstuffs, leave much to be desired. The
average Westerner is shocked at the widespread
squalor and filth found in all parts of China. The
Chinese do not have to be reminded of these evils,
however, and they take the necessary precautions
against diseases and epidemics by consuming nothing
but thoroughly-cooked and hot foods. If you go to
China and travel to the outskirts of the better cities,

you should take care to eat only native foods cooked thoroughly and served hot.

The Japanese eat raw fish and are very fond of it. Quite contrary to a popular Western misconception, however, they do not eat raw fish indiscriminately. I doubt if that has ever been the case. There are only certain kinds of fish which we consider suitable for eating raw. Japan is surrounded by friendly seas. Furthermore, except for one section of the main island of Honshu, there is no part of Japan more than fifty miles from the sea. Therefore, fish are plentiful and fresh. To eat raw fish Japanese style, the fish must first be sliced into small, thin pieces and then dipped into thick *shoyu,* or soy sauce, which has been mixed with horseradish or vinegar, depending on the kind of fish to be eaten.

To the Westerner, raw fish is an acquired taste. Although eating raw fish at first may sound outlandish, to the Japanese it is no different from eating raw oysters on the half shell. Dipping them into tomato catsup doesn't cook them. Just as oyster cocktail is expensive in most world centers, so is raw fish relatively so in Japan, for the fish have to be very fresh and of a dainty nature before we will buy them.

In addition to eating a few of them raw, fish are cooked in a hundred and one ways in Japan. In my country they occupy the same place that meat does in Western countries. They are either boiled or broiled. Lack of refrigeration forced the Japanese long ago to devise many odd ways of preserving fish.

66

Perhaps one of the most amazing marine products to Westerners is *katsuobushi* or dried bonito. After the bones of the fish are removed, it is sliced into three pieces, boiled, and then dried in drying ovens. The finished product, usually seven or eight inches long and an inch in diameter, looks more like a piece of wood than palatable food, for it is brown and hard and will keep for years. *Katsuobushi* is shaved into thin flakes and used for making soup stock. Also, these thin flakes are boiled in *shoyu,* salt, or sugar and made into a kind of fish-meal preserve, which the Japanese eat with rice.

Another popular sea product is dried squid or cuttlefish. Millions of squid are caught in the northern waters of Hokkaido and are dried in the sun. When dried the fish becomes like a thin piece of paper. Cut into small slices it is chewed by the Japanese like chewing gum.

A mere mention of octopus, let alone the thought of eating it, may give Westerners a creepy sensation. We Japanese, however, are very fond of octopus, slightly boiled, sliced, and the pieces dipped in vinegar. Octopus meat is rather gummy and hard to chew, but the Japanese like its peculiar taste. One curious fact is that the octopus is carnivorous; it feeds on small fish and shellfish after poisoning them. But when it has nothing to eat, it consumes its own tentacles, which soon grow again! In Japan, when a business firm has made no profit but pays dividends out of its capital, such a dividend is popularly called an "octopus dividend."

Fish does not seem to be considered a very satisfying food item in America, whereas the Japanese like fish for its simple but delicate taste. For some reason or other, fish caught in Japanese waters seem better tasting than those caught elsewhere. Many visitors to Japan have said the same thing. Mr. Joseph Grew, American ambassador to Japan before the war, writes of something to the same effect in his *Ten Years in Japan.*

Of course, the Japanese do not raise many cattle. We do not have land enough for such a purpose. We have to depend almost entirely on fish for our supplies of protein and calcium. In fact my countrymen have the habit of eating small fish including the bones in order to provide essential minerals in our diet.

It is remarkable how, over the course of thousands of years, the Japanese have explored all conceivable sources of marine flora and fauna for possible food items. *Kombu,* or kelp, which grows naturally in the sea-shallows of our northern waters, is used extensively in making soup stock and for cooking with other dishes. Many foreigners in Japan have learned to like it and to cook with it.

I once visited the northeastern tip of Hokkaido and found kelp-gathering a principal industry there. The promontory is immediately contiguous to the Kurile Island chain, now occupied by the Soviets through some provision of the Yalta Agreement, and constituting a stepping-stone to the Aleutians and thence into Alaska. The promontory is the Land's

End of Japan and is cold, bleak, and inhospitable. However, hardy fishermen go out to gather kelp along the rugged coast in small craft, which are at the mercy of the treacherous currents. Like San Francisco or London, in spite of changeable weather, it is foggy in this district almost all year around. In recent years a number of these kelp collectors have been arrested and held by the Soviets on the flimsiest of charges. The Soviet seize the men and their little hand-hewn boats and take them to a Russian patrol station on the Kuriles. Despite such obvious dangers, however, these fishermen must go out and gather kelp off the rugged, rocky coast, for they have no other way to make a living. Theirs is a life of constant struggle with nature in an effort to wrest a livelihood from the sea. However, they do not mind these natural dangers. Their life reminds me of an impressive British film I saw some years ago called *The Island of Arran*. The story was about a bleak, barren, and inhospitable island somewhere off the coast of Scotland, where the inhabitants had to put up a grim fight against all sorts of dangers and hardships in order to eke out a meager living. The Scottish people are known for their frugality and industry. These characteristics are in a large measure the result of their natural surroundings. The same conditions hold true for my countrymen, especially those who toil in our northern waters gathering kelp.

Japanese cooking is not confined to fish dishes. We also use beef and chicken as ingredients in some

69

of our dishes. But I hasten to add that what meat is used in such dishes is usually in tiny slices and does not amount to much. *Sukiyaki,* the beef and vegetable concoction favored by foreign visitors and of which the Japanese themselves are very fond, is probably the only dish in which meat is used in any considerable quantity. Nevertheless, beef consumed per person in a *sukiyaki* dinner is probably half the amount of meat in an ordinary steak dinner. The fascination in *sukiyaki* consists in the pleasure of the diners themselves preparing the food and eating it at the table—an extension of the kitchen to the parlor. There is not much culinary art involved in the preparation of *sukiyaki,* although the raw vegetables and meats to go into it are usually artistically served on colorful pottery. The dish was originated some eighty years ago, when the Japanese began to eat beef, so *sukiyaki* cannot be regarded as a time-honored Japanese dish.

Fish and vegetables constitute the main ingredients in Japanese cooking, and I may add that the color scheme and the arrangement on the dishes constitute the most outstanding features of Japanese food. The appetite of Japanese gourmets is stimulated through the eye. This fact will explain why all Japanese soups, except for the traditional soybean soup at breakfast, are clear. One can thereby admire the bits of flower-shaped vegetables and the pearly eye of a fish in the bottom of the bowl, which is made of black or red lacquer. Even a cook in a *yadoya,* or country inn, is mindful of such pleasing details of decoration. For example, he will cut carrots in the shape of maple leaves for soup as a reminder of a seasonal attraction.

Our cooks thus devote much attention to color scheme and arrangement so that the dishes can be a feast to the eye as well as to the palate. Some dishes, moreover, are designed to be a delight to the ear as well. We Japanese are like that! Pickled radish, which is as offensive to the noses of most foreigners as is cheese to the noses of some Japanese, is one of the most favorite side dishes, and goes well with boiled rice and green tea. Slices of well-pickled radishes are so crisp that we enjoy munching them with audible sound. Dried salmon roe is another favorite food item. It, too, is rather hard and crisp, and although it makes no audible noise, the Japanese enjoy eating it. *Udon,* a Japanese equivalent of spaghetti made of wheat flour, is a popular Japanese food. Prepared in diluted *shoyu* the Japanese eat this noodle with *éclat,* making considerable noise, sometimes reminding one of the noise of heavy rainfall.

Although it is considered bad manners in the West to make noises while eating or sipping, the Japanese do so, especially with soup. With us it is sometimes regarded as a mark of appreciation of the food or beverage. Whenever the members of our group touring the United States were invited to dinner by Americans, they nonchalantly made noises while partaking of soup or even coffee. The Americans were surprised. Knowing and appreciating the

71

difference in customs, I was ashamed of my country-men, but, fearing to offend them, I did not have the courage to warn them.

Just as with products of the sea, the Japanese have done everything possible to exploit what is edible on land. Bamboo sprouts are eaten with great relish, and chrysanthemum blossoms are either boiled or pickled and eaten as a delicacy. Tender green maple leaves are dipped in dough and fried in deep fat. With eighty-eight million people living in an extremely mountainous country with a very small area of arable land, stark necessity prompts a con-tinuous search for good eatables. The Japanese find pleasure and satisfaction in simplicity and have learned to love daintiness in small things. Such is true in many aspects of Japanese life. Rather than complain about their poverty they do the best they can with the little that Mother Nature has to offer.

Many Japanese foods, such as bamboo sprouts, octopus, and dried squid, are quite coarse to for-eigners and even to us, and are not easily digested. Through long years of biting and chewing coarse foods, the Japanese have developed protruding teeth. Although they have cultivated an innate taste for some of these native foods, the Japanese, especially the younger generation, would rather eat Western or Chinese food, which uses more meat and fat. In summer months, when it is extremely hot, the simple flavors of Japanese dishes are quite welcome, but normally preference is shown for the more satisfy-ing meals such as are served in Western-style restaurants. It is curious, however, that as Japanese grow old they prefer Japanese to Western food.

According to recent statistics, the average annual consumption of meat per person in Japan is only three pounds. This amazingly low average is explained by the fact that living standards vary widely between rural and urban areas. Whereas some city dwellers eat meat fairly frequently, farmers, even the relatively wealthy ones, subsist almost entirely on a vegetarian diet throughout the year. There is no Japanese counterpart to the American farmer who drives a motor car and eats the same food as city inhabitants.

The Japanese love of rice is both passionate and ingrained. They do not believe that any meal is really substantial without rice. They are like the Irish I read about, who, while building the railroads in America's great West, demanded meat and potatoes and more meat and potatoes every day. The average Japanese likes foreign food very much, but he still insists on having a bowl of rice at least once a day. In the final months of 1945, immediately after the surrender, the Japanese food situation was very critical. Many Japanese would have perished of hunger had it not been for the generous shipments of American wheat. This wheat was rationed to the general public, along with indigenous rice which the government bought from the farmers. Despite rationing, many people from the big cities went out into the country to hunt for black-market rice, for which they paid exorbitant prices. Severe penalties were meted out to those caught with black-market rice. The trains were overcrowded, and there were many tragic accidents. Nevertheless, the people, undaunted, sought rice, even at the risk of their lives, when they could get wheat much cheaper and more easily.

At Japanese receptions or buffet suppers to which foreigners are invited, the custom is to serve sandwiches, in addition to *sushi,* small rice balls flavored with vinegar and wrapped in seaweed. On such occasions the Japanese invariably take *sushi,* not caring for the sandwiches. Even American-born Japanese in California are said to be passionately fond of *sushi,* and many prefer it to sandwiches.

Japanese farmers consume large amounts of rice every day, mainly because they have so little else in the way of foods. The average Japanese farmer is so poor that he cannot even afford fish more than once or twice a month. He lives almost entirely on rice and vegetables grown on his farm. As a result, some farmers suffer from beriberi, a paralysis of the legs, caused by a vitamin deficiency. City people do not eat as much rice as farmers do, for they take more fish and meat. But no Japanese can do without rice, for it gives him a sense of fullness that no other food will give.

Foreigners watching the Japanese eat their native food are astonished at the speed with which the food is consumed. In fact, some groups—such as carpenters and laborers—make a point of devoting as little time as possible to their meals. Considering the fact that Japanese food is often coarse and indigestible, this speed is really remarkable. **Perhaps** this is a hangover from olden days, when warriors were urged to eat their meals with the utmost dispatch, since they might be called to battle at a moment's notice. Overpopulation may also be partly responsible for this habit of rapid eating. In a large family of perhaps a dozen children, a wild scramble for rice is natural, especially when it is apportioned on a "first come, first served" basis. This competition may have encouraged the Japanese to eat their meals quickly, and a convenient way to come out first is to pour green tea over the rice, so that it can be swallowed whole rather than masticated. The fact that diseases of the digestive organs are very prevalent among the Japanese may be attributed to this unwholesome habit and to the inordinate use of rice, pickles, and green tea.

One sees in Japanese cities many signs on hospitals and in front of doctors' homes showing specialization in stomach ailments. Our newspapers are full of advertisements of special pills and patent medicines for the cure of stomach and bowel troubles. The Japanese stomach is inordinately inflated, and its position is much lower than that of Westerners', mainly because of the heavier weight which rice imposes on the stomach. Also, the bowels of Japanese are, according to medical evidence, longer than those of Occidentals by a foot or so, because of the inveterate vegetarian diet.

I discarded rice-eating many years ago and have since "subsisted" entirely on Western food. Many of my Japanese friends have wondered how in the world I could do without rice for so many years. Some of them even think I am a bit odd and certainly an unhappy person for not eating such a delectable food! Once in a while I have to eat rice in the company of my countrymen, when there is nothing else to eat. Whenever I do so, I become sluggish and sleepy. I truly believe that the Japanese people would be more mentally alert if they refrained from eating so much rice.

Be that as it may, rice is a very economical staple food. If all Japanese switched from rice to bread, something most unlikely, the area of cultivatable land would not be sufficient to grow enough wheat to feed the population. The quantity of rice grown in a given area can feed twice as many people as can wheat or other grains grown in the same area. Moreover, with bread one needs butter and jam or other condiments, which Japanese farmers are unable to produce in any appreciable quantity, much less buy.

There is in Japan the so-called "sun-flag lunch," carried in a small tin box to work. It is so called because it consists of boiled rice with no other food except a tiny, red pickled plum buried in the center; the whole thing suggests the Japanese national flag, which shows a sun on a white background. To eat the "sun-flag lunch" is considered a laudatory example of frugality and austerity. What a contrast to the typical American lunch of sandwiches, a banana or sweets, and a thermos of hot coffee!

Lack of extensive pasture land has forced the Japanese to seek animal fat in other forms. Eel and *loche,* a snake-like creature, are typical examples of the result of this search. These are cultivated in lakes and lagoons in a sort of hatchery. Eel is broiled in soy sauce and eaten with rice. It is a rich and tasty food, and the Japanese are extremely fond of it. Incidentally, it is an expensive food. A story is told of a poor man who stood in front of an eel restaurant in which eels were being broiled. Eel is very odorous while being cooked, and the poor man was enjoying the delectable air wafting from the restaurant. Suddenly the proprietor of the restaurant, evidently a hardened money-grabber, came out and tried to charge the man for smelling and consuming the eel odors.

The Japanese like to go out to dine, and unlike most of the British, who stick to their own foods, they are epicures and gourmets. Tokyo and other big cities are jammed with restaurants, both large and small, Oriental and Occidental. Before the war, the best Japanese cooks of Western foods were mostly trained in the French style. The Nippon Yusen Kaisha, at that time one of the foremost steamship companies in the world, had excellent chefs, whose cooking was well known to travellers of many nationalities.

Western food in Japanese restaurants is prepared and served in orthodox European style, and consists of hors d'oeuvres, soup, fish, entree, and so on down the line. Usually, there is only a small

77

portion of each dish, but in first-class restaurants the servings are generous, excellently cooked, and delicious. After the war, as a result of thousands of Japanese being trained in American homes, many have learned American cooking.

American foodstuffs, also, are now available in Tokyo and other cities, although prices are very high. Like the Germans, the Japanese, especially the younger generation, are inveterate coffee drinkers. They would sacrifice almost anything for a cup of coffee. However, it is expensive in Japan, a cup of good coffee costing the equivalent of twenty cents, a price completely out of proportion to the fifty-dollar-a-month salary the average office worker receives. Nevertheless, young people flock to these numerous coffee shops at all times of the day.

The Japanese are also great between-meal nibblers. No more striking example of this can be given than when they board a train for a long ride. No sooner do the passengers take their seats than they start eating peanuts, fruits in season, and other things; and in less than half an hour the floors of the coaches are littered with peelings, waste paper, and other refuse, which these days are thrown indiscriminately about.

The Japanese conception of a floor is different from that of Westerners, I am sure. For centuries they have been used to living on a matted floor on which they would never dream of walking with their shoes on. Anywhere else, anywhere off the *tatami,* halls, floors, and the like, where they walk with their shoes on, is considered an extension of the public sidewalk, and as such one can throw his cigarette butt on it, or even spit on it, with impunity.

This habit of incessant nibbling between meals is presumably because regular meals are not always satisfying, nor very nourishing; hence the Japanese have to continue eating to fill their stomachs.

Japanese food, as I pointed out at the outset of this chapter, is the result of many years' experimentation on what is most suitable for the Japanese in terms of those materials which are readily available. The Japanese, therefore, go in for foreign food both because of its novelty and because of its more satisfying nature. In spite of this, the average Japanese will revert to his native meal of rice and fish whenever possible, especially in old age. Many Japanese travellers to the United States make serious efforts to visit Japanese restaurants in New York, Los Angeles, and San Francisco to enjoy their native food. They feel very miserable otherwise, for such is the inertia of humans regarding their eating habits.

5   Believe It or Not

WHEN a Japanese is asked "Is it hot?" he replies, "Yes, it is hot." When asked "Is it not hot?" he invariably replies, "Yes, it is not." It takes some time for a foreigner to get used to this apparently baffling mentality of the Japanese. In fact, it is better not to ask a Japanese a question in the negative, for he will answer "yes" irrespective of whether the question is in the affirmative or the negative.

Again, in the matter of writing, Japanese customs are quite the opposite of Western ones. We write from right to left and usually from the top of the page to the bottom. Japanese books end where Western ones begin, and footnotes are printed at the top of the page.

When writing addresses we start with the name of the country, e.g.: U.S.A., New York State, New York City, West 42nd Street, No. 153. When writing names the same procedure is followed—first the family name is written and then the middle and given name, with the honorific at the end, e.g.: Truman, S. Harry, Mr. In writing a letter the salutation, "Dear so and so," the date, etc., come at the end of the letter.

From the point of view of a Westerner, almost everything the Japanese do is topsy-turvy. When beckoning you to come they wave their hand toward you, palm out; when counting on their fingers they first stretch out all their fingers and then bend them down, one by one beginning with the thumb; when all the fingers are down at five, they turn up the little finger for six and go on from there.

When handing back change to a purchaser, the Japanese will first hand over the biggest note. In America if the change is say $1.40 the store clark hands over the nickel first, then the dime, followed by a quarter and finally the dollar bill. In Japan change is counted the opposite way. The dollar bill would be given first, then the quarter, the dime, and finally the nickel. In Japan the implication is that as long as you receive the major portion of the change, the dollar in this instance, the rest is considered relatively unimportant. As a matter of fact very few Japanese even count the small change when it is received, for to do so would be looked upon as a sure sign of parsimony.

Though generally poor, the Japanese pretend to be unconcerned about money matters. If there is any change to be paid between two friends, and the amount is small, the would-be receiver either declines to accept it or tells the other party to keep it. Japanese reluctance to discuss personal money affairs is such that when a Japanese goes out for a cup of coffee or lunch with several of his friends, one person usually pays the entire bill and seldom is there a settling-up afterward. One of my acquaintances, who had spent a good many years abroad, used to behave otherwise and he was branded a miser, although nothing could be farther from the truth in his case.

When Japanese carpenters saw or plane lumber, they pull the tools toward themselves. No Western carpenter would do this. Similarly, when striking a match or sharpening a pencil, they do it away from their bodies.

The Japanese umbrella is made of oiled paper on ribs of bamboo. When closed it is carried handle down by means of a ring or loop at the top.

In denoting directions the Japanese say "east-north" or "west-south" rather than "north-east" or "south-west."

Innumerable examples of such customs which are opposite to Western ways can be cited. In fact, if Occidentals assume that the Japanese generally do things the opposite way from them, they will probably not be far from wrong.

The Japanese do not seem to consider heating their houses in cold weather. The only source of heat inside the house is usually a small charcoal stove, which is used more for warming the hands than the room itself. Instead, the Japanese go out into the open and build a bonfire. Such a fire is made by burning stacks of straw, and as many people as possible cluster around the fire to warm their bodies. This type of fire is usually made on bleak wintery mornings before the start of the day's work. It is a very unsatisfactory method of heating for Westerners, I am sure, as the heat generated is soon dissipated into the air, and the smoke gets in your eyes. Moreover, as soon as the fire goes out everyone gets cold again. However, Japanese houses are not suitable for installing stoves, let alone fireplaces, since they are too flimsily built. In any case, the average Japanese would be too poor to afford a stove in his house, since fuel is scarce and expensive.

When I travelled on the Trans-Siberian Railway in 1946 from Moscow to Vladivostok, I saw countless Japanese POW camps established along this long and famous railway. Here and there I saw people making bonfires in the open spaces to warm themselves with, and I knew instinctively that they were my countrymen. I did not know whether the Russians would not allow the Japanese prisoners to heat their camps or whether the Japanese were merely following their peculiar native habit.

I have already explained at length what enjoyment the Japanese derive from a bath. To them taking a bath is such an exhilarating experience that they will go to great lengths to get one. In Western countries a bath is merely a means to cleanse one's body. In Japan the people do not object to taking a bath several times a day. As a matter of fact this is often done by people staying at hotspring resorts.

When visiting a friend's house, the host often invites the caller to take a bath as soon as he arrives. This is looked upon as a great hospitality, comparable to an invitation to stay for dinner. In the West, such an invitation would be regarded as an affront, implying that the visitor is so dirty that he needs a bath.

At a formal dinner party in Japan, before the dinner starts, the host delivers a speech, to which the principal guest responds. And at such a party the Japanese do not serve one dish after another as is done in the West; rather most of the dishes are already placed on the tray long before the dinner commences. Only soup, rice, and special items are brought in after the dinner starts. The "pre-dinner" speech is exceedingly annoying to most guests, especially when they are hungry. The appetizing dishes so beautifully arranged on the tray in front of you are most tantalizing; but no one is supposed to touch them until the speeches are over. By that time some of the dishes are already quite cold, although the Japanese as a rule do not mind cold food.

The institution of after-dinner speeches in the West seems more logical in timing than the Japanese practice of pre-dinner speeches, for you have already enjoyed the meal and drinks by the time the speakers start to make their speeches and you have nothing else to do but relax, listen, and ponder the remarks. This timing is logical from the listeners' point of view. However, the prospective speaker at a Western dinner party might welcome the Japanese practice, since he would be through with his speech before he started eating, and hence would undoubtedly enjoy his own dinner more.

Perhaps I am contributing to Ripley's "Believe It or Not" by enumerating these various Japanese practices which seem so topsy-turvy to Westerners. I should like to mention one other remarkable aspect of a Japanese dinner: the host usually runs away before the guests have taken their leave! This un-Western-like practice is a result of the fact that Japanese dinners are seldom given at home. They are held at teahouses or restaurants and are usually stag affairs. Actually there is no host in the strict sense of the term, nor a hostess, to see to it that the menu is proper or that the flowers are in order. Such details are left to the management of the establishment, the host merely indicating beforehand how much he is willing to pay for the evening. Furthermore, most people give parties at somebody else's expense nowadays, and few pay out of their own pockets. Ironically enough the invited guests are almost always aware of this fact.

Such being the case, a dinner party is a sort of organized attempt by everyone concerned to get tipsy and be merry. Some parties end up in a little wild revelling. The guests, feeling the effects of the alcohol, like to stay on and spend as much time at the inn as they can, usually in the company of the geisha hostesses. The host, therefore, does not wish to mar the happy mood of his guests, nor does he want to stay on indefinitely until they all leave. Hence his sudden disappearance! Also he may perhaps be a busy man, with other engagements, or having to make the rounds of other parties. The Japanese dinner party, therefore, is more like a Western cocktail party, in that guests can take leave whenever they wish. But nowhere else in the world is the host permitted to leave the party that he himself is giving before the invited guests start going home.

The way the Japanese present a gift is also somewhat different from the Western practice. When visiting friends, the Japanese usually takes with him a gift of some sort which he presents at the conclusion of the visit. The gift is usually wrapped in paper, and the recipient is not supposed to open it in the presence of the donor. When presenting his gift, the donor apologizes for the smallness of the gift, saying that the article is valueless, or that it is hardly worth being accepted, or the like. The recipient, on his part, contradicts such remarks promptly by saying that he is extremely touched by the expression of such kindness as shown in the act of presenting the gift, although he does not know what the contents of the package are. The Japanese avoids causing embarrassment to the donor by not opening the package in the latter's presence, in case the gift happens to be of a mediocre or unsatisfactory nature.

The British people are known for their quality of understatement. The Frenchman's *"Ça, c'est magnifique"* is often equivalent to the Englishman's "It is not bad at all." The Japanese also deny themselves the satisfaction of self-expression and delight in understatement.

Gifts should never be presented ostentatiously. Japanese politeness demands this. However, the Western custom of opening the package on the spot and praising the gift and, if it happens to be an edible, of partaking of the gift with the donor seems a more spontaneous and much more pleasant custom.

The Japanese makes a point of expressing thanks to his host or donor the next time both meet after the gift or dinner favor was received. Japanese often wonder why Westerners fail to do the same.

Incidentally, when making a monetary gift a Japanese often puts the money in an envelope. Even a tip, other than that given to a railroad porter and such people, is enclosed in a small envelope especially made for the purpose. In Japan, checks are not generally used in daily life, and even the monthly salary of workers is invariably paid in cash. Such cash is almost always enclosed in an envelope, so that in Japan instead of pay check the word "pay envelope" is used. This practice of enclosing gifts of money in envelopes is derived from our disinclination to deal too openly with money matters. Few take the trouble of examining the contents of the envelope when it is received, for to do so would betray bad manners. Also, they would want to avoid the embarassment of showing disappointment, in case the money in the envelope is less than they expected.

Another instance of doing things backward takes place at a Japanese inn. When staying at a hotel it is not customary for the guest to ask for rates when he registers. Perhaps he will indicate generally the sort of accommodation he requires, whether first class, medium, or what-have-you, but he will never ask the hotel manager how much he will have to pay for the room and meals, nor will the management say anything about it. Consequently, a guest at a Japanese inn is kept in the dark as to the amount of the bill he will be asked to pay until it is actually presented at the end of his stay.

It is considered ill-mannered to discuss money matters at an inn, where the innkeeper is supposed to offer his best hospitality regardless of how much he will be paid for it. Of course, the guest has to pay for the services rendered but should on no account inquire or argue about the rates upon his arrival. As would be expected, this custom sometimes gives rise to embarrassing situations.

Tipping—although a nuisance in Japan, as it is elsewhere—is not very widespread. In a Japanese hotel you do not have to worry about tipping each and every person who may lay his hands on your baggage, or those who serve your meals. Gratuities for the hotel employees are included in the hotel bill. Elsewhere tipping is hardly a problem, except when travelling on the railroads. Here again, however, porters and train stewards are not half as expectant or insistent as their American counterparts.

At a Japanese-style hotel the guest behaves quite differently from the way he does in a Western-style hotel. By far the biggest difference is that in a Japanese hotel one takes his meals, writes letters, reads, and lounges in a private room; and brushes his teeth,

89

gargles, and bathes in a common room. The Japanese inn, or *yadoya*, is devoid of a dining room. Meals are brought into the private room of the guest on a small tray by a maid. The individual hotel room has no bathing or washing facilities. It is a familiar morning sight in a Japanese inn to see the guests walking up and down the hallway, looking disheveled and unkempt and often in pajamas, and proceeding to a common washroom, where they jostle each other while gargling, blowing their noses, or brushing their teeth, to the mutual annoyance of all concerned. This same Japanese, however, if he stayed in a Western-style hotel in Japan, would wash in the privacy of his room and come down to the dining room for meals and to the lounge for reading and chatting.

Speaking of the practice of cleaning one's teeth, here is another example of our opposite way of doing things. The Japanese brush their teeth generally in the morning, in contrast with the Western habit of cleaning the teeth before retiring. Japanese toothpaste manufacturers have for many years encouraged the Japanese to clean their teeth both before retiring at night and after arising in the morning; some people have followed this sensible advice. However, most Japanese, perhaps nine out of ten, still prefer to clean their teeth only in the morning. One reason for this is the lack of hot and cold running water in most Japanese houses. In winter water has to be specially heated on a charcoal fire in the morning for washing. With icy cold water there is little inducement to clean the teeth at night before going to bed.

When building a house the Japanese make a great fuss about which direction the house should face. Common sense dicates that a house facing south and sheltered on the north is the best, in order to get the maximum sunshine, especially in Japan, where heating is almost nonexistent. But most Japanese go beyond that and consult a fortuneteller to ascertain which direction would be the luckiest one in which to build their house. They are especially particular about the location of the gate and the kitchen. The decision for both is usually made on the basis of time-honored superstition.

Little attention has ever been paid to sidewalks and zoning in Japan. Houses are built in haphazard fashion on any available lot, with little regard to the street or sidewalk. Residential districts in the outskirts of Tokyo are notorious for the haphazard and disorderly manner in which the streets, if they can be called streets at all, are numbered. Usually street names are not of the thoroughfares themselves but of the sections through which the streets run. For example, No. 2 Cherry Street might be a block on which perhaps twenty-five houses and shops, both large and small, are clustered. It is often that one spends the better part of half an hour trying to locate Mr. Tanaka's house in No. 2 district. Adjacent to No. 2 may be No. 15 Cherry Street, where may be found another unmethodical conglomeration of perhaps sixteen houses with tortuous crisscrossing lanes. Again, No. 24 Cherry Street may be found in the immediate neighborhood, and so on. Streets and sidewalks often exist only in name; they are more often than not muddy, uneven paths, sometimes with pools of odorous sewage water flooding them. I have often spent over an hour frantically trying to locate the house of a friend in such a neighborhood. To make matters worse, neighbors are often unsociable; sometimes they do not even know the names of people living only a few doors away. This is a surprising fact which can be explained only by the extreme insularity of the average Japanese family.

Zoning is a subject to which Japanese city planners have given little thought. It is quite common to find a group of slummy wooden shacks of laborers immediately adjacent to the palatial residence of a millionaire. A man might build a beautiful house in what is considered a desirable residential section at the time of construction; but sooner or later shoddy houses might be built all around it, with the result that the value of the property would depreciate.

It is true that Japan is an old country and that houses in some districts might have been built many years ago when there was no such thing as city planning even in the West. It is also a very crowded country where there is not an inch of land that can be called valueless. Nevertheless, in the wake of a major disaster, such as an earthquake or a fire, when the greater part of a city is destroyed, there is an opportunity to modernize the city. However, few city planners have been courageous enough to avail themselves of such opportunities.

The American method of constructing roads and

sidewalks before houses are built at all could not be copied in an extremely crowded country like Japan. But roads and sidewalks in urban areas could be straightened out and improved, if only city officials had a little more courage and vision. Indifference of the residents to improving roads is equally astonishing. On a rainy day inhabitants are often seen wading through unpaved paths, splashing mud and ruining their shoes, and yet they never clamor for better roads. In the meantime, local government officials go on padding their expense accounts and whiling away their time sipping tea and drinking saké at banquets, unknowingly financed by the taxpayers.

The story of the topsy-turvyism of the Japanese people would not be complete without mentioning the well-known fact that in Japan men are definitely considered the superior sex; entering or leaving a room or building and on the street, the man precedes the woman. He is served his meals first. When taking a bath at home, priority is given the male members of the family, and the women, including the wife and daughters, have to wait until the men are through. Chivalry in the Western sense is little understood in Japan. Man's superiority over women derives principally from the feudalistic notion that women are supported by men, and that the woman's duty is to bring up the children and keep the house. Under such circumstances there is little difference between wife and maidservant.

While such a feudalistic social system is bound

to change in the long run, it will be many years before any appreciable progress can be made along Western lines.

6 How to Live on $50 a Month

WITH a teeming and expanding population having to share meager natural resources, the living standard of the average Japanese has been perennially low, except for about twenty years between the two world wars, when the Japanese people enjoyed relative affluence. Four years of relentless war in which Japan staked everything and lost naturally brought havoc to the Japanese economy, with the result that the Japanese today are pauperized.

Wars, like revolutions, are a great levelling factor. There is no doubt today that the nobles and the rich of prewar years are in greatly reduced circumstances. There is a great deal of outward show of prosperity by the privileged few, as exemplified by the large number of sleek, shining limousines seen on Tokyo streets today. Actually, judged by prewar standards, there are few really wealthy people today. However, by far the most outstanding result of defeat in the war has been the elimination of the so-called middle class. Before the war we had a solid middle class, which formed the backbone of the nation. Today these people are so reduced in circumstances that they can no longer be called middle class. Of course, they do not go about the streets in rags, but they are nevertheless paupers, in the sense that they live more or less from hand to mouth.

During the Occupation, I was asked one day by a group of high-ranking American army officers to conduct them on a tour of a Japanese movie studio. Japan had before the war, as now, a flourishing domestic movie industry, and the studio, though a mere toy affair compared with Hollywood studios, was interesting in its own way. After being shown through the paraphernalia used in Japanese film production, the American visitors wanted to see what a domestic Japanese film looked like. So I arranged with the management to have a modern Japanese picture of prewar vintage shown in the screening room. It was a picture made around 1935 depicting, among other things, the daily life of the Japanese. A middle-class Japanese family is shown drinking imported Scotch whisky, eating chocolates from fancy boxes, and living in a well-heated foreign-style annex of a Japanese house. The Japanese in those days, although not many of them possessed motor cars of their own, could easily afford to ride in taxis, which were ubiquitous, without worrying about the fare. They ate sumptuous meals then compared with what

96

they eat today. My American friends were very impressed by the relatively high standard of living enjoyed by the average Japanese in those days, for they had only seen and known the misery and poverty of the people since the war.

Another example of the affluence of the middle class before the war can be found in those Western-style houses in Tokyo and other cities, most of which are now being occupied by foreigners. In prewar years a university professor or army colonel could afford to build such a house and live there himself. Today the owners find these houses so expensive to maintain that they must either sell them or rent them to foreigners.

Although the standard of living of the average Japanese deteriorated steadily since the war, it has today been somewhat stabilized. There are indications that, barring unforeseen developments, living conditions will improve somewhat with gradual improvement in the Japanese economy. However, there can be little hope for a marked improvement in our standard of living, since any gains made in economic rehabilitation are offset by the rapid and constant increase in the population. The present low standard of living in Japan, therefore, may be expected to last for some time to come, and may be safely considered a constant factor in any discussion of the immediate problems of postwar Japan.

The disastrous effects of the defeat on the Japanese economy can be gauged by the value of Japanese currency today in terms of dollars. For many years before the war one U.S. dollar was equal to two Japanese yen; it was down to ¥3.70 immediately before the war. Today one dollar is officially quoted at ¥360 but may actually be worth ¥400 or more.

The mean wage scale for government employees is fixed at present at ¥12,000 a month. Business and industrial circles have adopted a corresponding wage scale. The income of an average salaried man with a wife and three children would come to ¥18,000 a month, including sundry allowances. The wage rate in many fields is even lower than this government wage scale. Now ¥18,000 in terms of American money is about $50. How a Japanese with a family of four or five can live on the paltry sum of $50 a month is something of a miracle.

It is commonly believed that the low cost of living in Japan tends to equalize the low scale of wages, making it possible for the Japanese salaried man to enjoy about the same comforts and opportunities as are enjoyed by his opposite numbers in other lands. This is one of the many misconceptions about Japan. The problem of making both ends meet is, for ninety per cent of my countrymen, something which must be handled not only by extreme thrift but also by much self-denial. Japanese periodicals devoted to women's interests are full of discussions of the problem, and symposiums are often held by housewives on the subject of how to eke out a living on their husbands' meager incomes.

Likewise, there is a popular semi-monthly publication printed in Tokyo which enjoys a large circulation among salaried men. The journal is full of articles with such alluring titles as "How to Save ¥1,000,000" ($2,900 in American currency, a sum representing a handsome fortune to the average Japanese); "How to Become a Millionaire from Scratch"; "Investment Strategy for 1955"; and so forth. Writers of these articles exhort people to exert systematic and almost superhuman efforts to save. I know that the average American would be aghast at such radical efforts to stint.

It must not be thought that everything is cheaper in Japan than in America. Rice, the staple food, costs slightly less in Japan, whereas wheat and sugar are more expensive, since these items have to be imported from abroad. Meat may be a little cheaper in Japan; a pound of beef of good quality, for example, costs about eighty cents. Proximity to the source of supply makes fish a cheap article of diet. On the other hand, butter, cheese, and milk are more expensive in Japan. Eggs are cheaper, the best grade selling for about fifty cents a dozen, but this is not an accurate comparison, for eggs in Japan are generally much smaller. Vegetables, as a rule, are cheaper in Japan, though the difference is not great.

Most items other than daily necessities are extremely dear. Coffee, cocoa, and such items are imported from abroad and are sold at a large margin of profit. A pound can of coffee costs ¥900 or $2.50, while other imported items are correspondingly expensive.

The average Japanese, with a monthly wage

of $50, therefore cannot afford to eat a dinner approximating in quality even an American breakfast. Consequently, they fall back on native food items, which are cheap and more palatable to the average Japanese. The typical menu of a Japanese household differs somewhat according to season, but the following will give a general idea:

Breakfast: Rice; *miso,* or thick bean soup with vegetables; *tsukudani,* preserved small fish, shell fish, or seaweed in soy sauce; and green tea.

Lunch: Rice; boiled or roasted fish; boiled dressed vegetables; and green tea.

Dinner: Rice; clear soup with *tofu,* or bean curd, and Japanese green onions; fried fish, boiled vegetables; pickles; and green tea.

The cost of these meals is somewhere around ¥80 or twenty-three cents per person per day; so the monthly food bill for a family of five could, with constant effort, be kept within $35.

Joining military service in Japan, as in other Asiatic countries, often results in an increased living standard for the individual concerned. Most recruits come from poor peasant or urban families and are better fed in the camps and barracks than at home. The Japanese National Self-Defense Corps, created for the defense of the nation, spends ¥3500 or roughly $9 per capita per month for food, so the diet is naturally more balanced and substantial than the fare of the average Japanese.

The Japanese are very fond of eating out. Government offices and business and industrial concerns frequently hold banquets on one pretext or another. For example, when a new section chief is appointed, the entire staff of that section, from the head down to lowest clerk, go out to some restaurant and hold a banquet to commemorate the occasion. None of the participants, including the chief himself, pay a cent for the party. All the expenses are paid out of a special fund allocated for the use of that particular section.

If an American agricultural expert happens to be visiting Tokyo, for instance, he may be sure to receive an invitation from the Agriculture Ministry, requesting the pleasure of his company at a Japanese dinner "in order to hear his valued opinion," the usual phraseology of a Japanese invitation card. The American visitor, if he attends such a party, will find much to his surprise a large Japanese gathering from the Minister of Agriculture down to the chiefs of the various bureaus and sections of the ministry. The dinner is always sumptuous and is quite a convivial affair with a great deal of saké-drinking, and with the celebrators invariably being waited upon by scores of geisha.

It is not exceptional at a Japanese party such as this for the hosts to far outnumber the guests! None of the hosts pays for the party out of his own pocket, and since the bill, no matter how staggering

101

in amount, will be charged to an expense account and paid anyway, those even remotely connected with the host claim equal rights of attendance.

Many high-ranking government officials and business executives in Japan spend almost every night at teahouses and restaurants attending banquets of some sort and seldom dine at home. It is a convenient way to make up for the caloric deficiency of their household meals. Because Japanese parties are essentially stag affairs, our poor wives and children have to stay at home and subsist on twenty-three-cent meals of rice, fish, and pickles.

It is one of those numerous Japanese incongruities that the Japanese, who spend so little on their meals at home, are lavish and wasteful at dinner parties. A fairly good dinner at an ordinary restaurant costs upward of ¥1,500, or $4, per person, exclusive of drinks. This sum represents just about half the total monthly food bill of the average Japanese. The Japanese are very fond of their native beer, and at such parties they open one bottle after another in rapid succession, without regard to their actual need or capacity, and leave most of the bottles half-empty. This wasteful habit cannot be condoned merely because the bill is to be charged to the expense account of the office.

The Japanese, as I have pointed out elsewhere, though frugal, are at the same time a very wasteful people. I have often wondered why Japanese organizations, instead of holding such lavish banquets as I have described, do not distribute such funds equally among their employees, so as to add to their general welfare and happiness.

The problem of housing today is still seriously affected by the severe wartime bombings and cannot be gauged by any normal standard. A Japanese wage earner with his monthly $50 may spend perhaps one-third of this income for house rent. A house renting for $15 could not conceivably be duplicated in America. It is a small hut of a very light construction, which gives no protection from the cold of winter. Its nearest counterpart would be a single room in a frame tenement. Considering the fact that the renter in Japan does not have the benefit of proper sewage disposal or improved streets or sidewalks, rents in Japan are not outstandingly cheaper than in America.

Electricity, gas, coal, and wood are very expensive in Japan. A family with a budget of $50 a month would have no more than a couple of electric lamps of 16-candle power and no heat other than a tiny charcoal fire. Heating being a luxury, it would be frightfully expensive to heat a house as in America. I know an American family living in a remodeled Japanese house of five small rooms in Tokyo. They use both gas and electric stoves for heating, and their monthly gas and electric bills during the winter months run up to ¥50,000, or nearly $150.

Western-style houses are in short supply in Japan because of wartime destruction and the great influx of foreign businessmen into the country since the war. Rents for such houses are usually much higher than for similar houses in America, and they have fewer amenities and facilities.

Streetcar and train fares are cheaper in Japan. A streetcar ride without transfer privileges is three cents in Tokyo and other large cities. A subway ride is four cents in Tokyo and Osaka. One can travel from Tokyo to Osaka, a distance of 350 miles on the government-operated railroads, for ¥700, or $1.90. But this is the minimum fare in a third-class coach on a slow train, which is often crowded and dingy. If one wishes to travel the same distance in any comfort, with a sleeper accommodation equivalent to a Pullman, the all-inclusive fare would be ¥7,500, or $21, which is by no means cheap compared with fares on American railroads.

The Japanese depend a great deal on railways, since motor transportation is deficient. Many people commute to work by train every day, but a monthly commutation ticket is by no means cheap by Japanese standards. Its purchase will make a serious dent in an already slender budget; therefore, most Japanese employers reimburse their workers for the monthly train fare.

Complimentary passes are issued liberally by both the government and the private railway companies in Japan, so that a large number of people travel free on the railroads. Passes are issued mainly to those who are connected with operation and management of the railways. But members of Parliament, high government dignitaries, and others demand and obtain free passes on one pretext or another. Possession of a complimentary railroad pass in Japan is equivalent to owning a Cadillac or Lincoln in America, for it will entitle the holder to travel first class on any line anywhere in the country, and even the remotest spot is accessible by train quite quickly, since Japan has a fine network of government-operated railroads throughout the country.

It is difficult to compare the cost of clothing in America and Japan, owing to the great difference in requirements. Cotton and silk textiles formerly cost much less in Japan than in America, but this is not necessarily the case today. Cotton yarn has to be imported from America and other countries and, unlike the prewar years, has to be shipped in foreign bottoms, with greater shipping cost. Of course, the Japanese cotton spinning industry still enjoys the advantage of comparatively cheap labor and high efficiency, but the lesser cost of the cotton fabric is largely offset by its inferior quality.

Most Japanese silk is earmarked for export, with the result that domestic silk prices are quite high. Wool is imported solely from Australia, and woolen fabrics processed in Japan are just as expensive as in other countries. As a matter of fact, the tendency in postwar years has been for prices of such international commodities as silk, wool, and cotton to become gradually equalized throughout most of the world.

Native Japanese kimono, contrary to popular

105

belief, is more expensive than European-style clothing, and many Japanese are adopting foreign-style
dress for reasons of economy. From personal experience I would say that a Western suit costs slightly
less in Japan than in America; the cost of woolen
material is about the same, so the saving is mainly
in the cost of tailoring. Japanese tailors charge $20
to $30 to cut and sew a suit of clothes, which I know
is substantially less than that charged by American
tailors.

Therefore, the average Japanese, with his
monthly income of $50, has to forego the pleasure of
a new suit and make maximum use of whatever
prewar clothes he might have. In recent years,
enterprising merchants have imported large quanti-
ties of secondhand clothing from the United States
and have been doing a thriving business. Before
the war the Japanese used to wear European-style
suits of tight jackets, vests, and trousers. Today
more and more Japanese are seen dressed in American-style clothing. During the winter months,
Japanese men, while wearing Western-style suits,
often wear thick cotton or woolen underwear, which
sometimes can be seen bulging out at the sleeves
and ankles. This is necessitated by their having to
live in unheated houses and also by their rather
low body temperature. Though Japanese winters
are quite rigorous, during the greater part of the
year the climate is so mild that little clothing is
needed, and lower-class people go about in shirt
sleeves in summer months. Clothing, nevertheless,

is quite a big item in a Japanese household budget.

The Japanese are able to live on their pitifully small incomes mostly because they do without many things which Westerners, particularly Americans, believe to be necessities. Moreover, there are certain clever tricks which, though they may seem petty and mean to the Westerner, make up for the meagerness of their incomes. Most Japanese office workers, either government officials or business clerks, go on frequent field trips. Japanese Government offices and business or industrial concerns allocate in their budgets each year sizable sums of money for travelling expenses. A Tokyo business firm might send one of its staff members to inspect its branch office in Kobe. A high central government official may be sent to Osaka to confer with local government officials on certain matters. There may of course be a genuine need for such trips, but more often than not these field trips are mere pretexts, especially in the case of government officials. Those who go on these so-called field trips are paid a lump sum for travelling expenses according to a set scale. These expenses are rather liberally computed, and there is usually room for economy. A petty clerk is paid for second-class train travel, but actually he will travel by third class, so that the difference is his own. He may be given travelling expenses to cover a week's journey, but may cut his trip short by a few days and thereby save money. Thus, field trips mean an extra source of income for salaried people.

In rural areas, especially prefectural offices,

this practice has occasionally degenerated into a racket. I know a section chief of a prefectural government who goes on field trips on an average of at least two weeks during a month. The income he derives from this source exceeds his official salary of $50. Often there are cases of flagrant dishonesty and outright fraud. A certain prefectural governor goes on field trips in his limousine, which incidentally is not his own but is provided by his office, along with a chauffeur and gasoline. The governor, however, makes it a point to put in a request to his finance section for reimbursement of travelling expenses as if he had travelled by train between the capital city and the field destination.

It may sometimes happen that funds allocated for travelling expenses have not all been used up by the end of the fiscal year. In such a case, there is a scramble for the funds. Everyone in the department sends in a fictitious travel schedule and collects his travelling expenses. All these things, however, are usually taken for granted, and a discreet silence is maintained from the governor on down, for everyone in the office is a beneficiary, potential or otherwise; the only losers are the poor taxpayers!

Employees in Japanese offices are often seen avidly reading newspapers during a great part of their duty hours. Most Japanese offices subscribe to various newspapers for the benefit of their staff members. The Japanese are great newspaper readers, and in Tokyo alone there are at least half a dozen leading dailies. The average Japanese subscribes to one daily paper at home, for although he would like to read many more he cannot afford it. So the office caters to the rest of his needs. Subscription rates for a Japanese daily newspaper are only ¥150, or 40 cents a month, the price of just one copy of an American periodical.

There are in Japan a tremendous number of bookstores and magazine stalls, for the number of periodicals and books published in Japan is extraordinarily large. The Japanese read magazines and periodicals with great zeal. However, most of them cannot afford to buy as many books and periodicals as they would like, so they go to these stores and peruse the magazines displayed on the shelves. Some avid readers even read the entire contents of a periodical this way. Most bookstores are thronged with this type of visitor, who remains as long as half an hour in the store, reading the various books and magazines. The proprietors, however, do not show—at least outwardly—much displeasure at this type of reader, for to do so would drive away potential purchasers of their wares. They also write off the display copy of each magazine displayed, for it is usually too soiled to be sold to a customer. In a way, this custom of allowing the public to freely indulge in reading in the store is good advertising, attracting a large potential clientele.

The Japanese are passionately fond of hot-spring baths, but very few people except the very wealthy can afford trips to hotspring resorts. So at least twice a year Japanese offices conduct trips to

109

such resorts for the benefit of their staffs. If the office is a large one, its various sections and departments organize weekend outings separately at the expense of the entire organization. The Japanese are a gregarious people and enjoy immensely such collective outings. But here again, no attention is paid to the poor wives and children, who must stay at home.

It is customary for government offices and business firms to pay their employees the equivalent of at least one month's pay at the end of the year as a special bonus. This is a time-honored practice, for Japanese employees in former times had to work long, hard hours, not resting on Sunday or other holidays. But the employers granted them at least two holidays during the year, each of which of several days' duration: one at mid-year, when there was usually a family reunion to revere their ancestors; and the other at New Year's, which is the most celebrated of all Japanese holidays. On these two occasions employees were always given a certain amount of money with which to enjoy their well-earned holiday. These semi-annual bonuses, especially the one at year-end, have been an important supplementary source of income for Japanese workers, whose salaries are so notoriously meager.

The American authorities during the Occupation could not see the point when the Japanese Finance Ministry sought authorization to pay government employees a year-end bonus of the equivalent of a month's pay. The American officials argued that the monthly salary should be of such an amount as to enable the employee to live on it without requiring such a large bonus. If the Japanese Government had sufficient financial resources to pay each of its employees an extra month's salary, why didn't the government proportionately increase each employee's monthly salary? The Japanese pleaded that New Year's was a festive occasion to which much importance was attached, and that the holiday season occasioned greater expenses than in normal months. This was not a particularly convincing argument, inasmuch as the Americans also needed much money for Christmas, yet they did not receive an extra month's pay in December. The point of view of the Japanese is that the monthly salary of the average worker is so low that it is not possible to save anything out of it for the holiday season, hence the need for a year-end bonus.

I have pointed out that in the Japanese worker's monthly salary of $50, there is no room whatever for the purchase of clothing. So with his special bonus at the end of the year he is able to buy a pair of secondhand trousers for say $6 or a new overcoat for $25. Furthermore, this year-end bonus system is very flexible. As a general rule, the equivalent of one month's salary is paid, especially in the case of government workers. But many business firms, when business is good, pay as much as the equivalent of two or three months' salary. The bonus, therefore, serves as an incentive to the employees.

Thus there are several factors to compensate

for the amazingly low Japanese wage scale. However, it must not be thought that everyone has the benefit of these indirect and supplementary payments. Small business firms, for example, are unable to pay their employees even a basic salary of $50. A domestic servant, whose pay is somewhere around $6 a month with food and lodging, cannot hope to receive any supplementary income and, unlike his Chinese counterpart, does not usually stoop to the practice of "squeeze." So the majority of Japanese have to make strenuous efforts to live on their pitifully small incomes.

Yet, due to the influence of Buddhism, the Japanese by and large have been rather indifferent to money matters and do not worry too much about their poverty. They consider themselves lucky if they do not starve in this land of scarcity and congestion. In olden days Tokyo inhabitants used to boast of not spending money carried over from the previous day. Whatever money one made during the day was better spent on the same day, for who knows what tomorrow will bring in this country where natural calamities are of almost daily occurrence. A characteristic scorn for money is mingled with a fatalistic philosophy, which again is largely a product of Buddhism. Buddhism preaches that all temporal things are ephemeral and that real happiness lies in another world. Why then should you stint and save when you cannot take it with you to the other world? Such, briefly, is their philosophy.

Even today, talk of money matters is generally

scorned and to be avoided as much as possible. Perfectly legitimate means of augmenting one's income by buying and selling stocks and shares on the Stock Exchange has been, and still is, widely deprecated.

The Japanese are generally modest in their personal desires and ambitions. Even a successful business executive does not want more than a small country house with a garden to retire to as the answer to his cherished desire. A private yacht, a country estate, and a round-the-world cruise are things even a Japanese millionaire never dreams of having.

The United Nations recently published data on national wealth of the principal countries of the world, throwing an interesting sidelight on the subject of national income. According to the statistics, the annual income per capita in America is $1,500, followed by Sweden with $800, Great Britain, $600, Germany, $400, while the mean annual income per capita in Japan is $150.

Thus, the ratio of per capita income between America and Japan, according to the United Nations report, is ten to one. A member of the so-called middle class in Japan makes $50 a month, while his counterpart in the United States would make $500, which seems to me to be approximately correct.

7   Bespectacled Dwarfs

NO less an authority on Japan than Alfred West said that the Japanese are good in small things and small in good things. In spite of its irony, I am, at times, impressed with this view. The Japanese are a small race, and although these physical characteristics are primarily hereditary, the vegetarian diet and peculiar mode of living have also exerted an important influence.

Occidental visitors to Japan, accustomed to Western practices, are surprised to find the position of the wash basins in trains and other places so low that they find it uncomfortable to use them. Similarly, they find the men's urinals ridiculously low. In prewar years the only chairs foreigners found at all comfortable were those in the Imperial Hotel and in a few other Western-style hotels in the larger

115

cities. In general, Japanese-made chairs and tables, dressers and furniture have such short legs that even Japanese who are used to Western-style living find them extremely awkward.

The Japanese are short in stature largely on account of their legs being so short. One often sees ungainly people in Japan, one-third of whose stature consists of the legs while their trunks and heads constitute two-thirds of their height. Even well-developed, shapely Japanese have proportionately shorter legs than Occidentals.

Because of such short legs Japanese women, more often than not, look ungainly in Western dress. Their native kimono conceals this kind of unsightly physique. One reason for the proportionately longer body seems to be the inflated stomach and elongated bowels to which a vegetarian diet over a long period of time has given rise. If their legs developed to about the same length as the upper part of the body, the Japanese would be quite tall. Because of their physical appearance, many Japanese suffer from inferiority feelings when associating with Westerners. However intelligent he may be, the average Japanese experiences a certain handicap when talking to people who tower over him as the average American or European does. He will at least feel a physical strain under such conditions. When travelling abroad, he is inclined to be self-conscious because of his physique and also because he is unaccustomed to Western manners and customs. The Japanese habit of over-tipping while travelling abroad is well known. In

France and in Italy, where tipping is such a nuisance, waiters in hotels and restaurants are very anxious to serve Japanese, for they know how generously they tip.

A recent Japanese visitor to the United States, a mayor of a provincial town who had never been abroad before, had an amusing experience. Wanting a haircut, he went into a barbershop in Chicago. He did not speak English, about the only English word he knew being "O.K.," which he had the habit of using rather indiscriminately. The barber asked the mayor first whether he wanted a haircut, to which he replied "O.K." He was then asked whether a shampoo was necessary, and the reply was the same. The next question was if the mayor wanted hair tonic. He said "O.K." and was given it! That question was followed by whether the customer desired a lotion sprinkled on his face. Out came "O.K.," and he was thoroughly sprinkled! His repeating of the only English word he knew could not be stopped, and he spoke it again when asked if he needed a massage! The total bill came to $7.00, which the mayor paid without protest. He tipped an extra dollar on top of that. The mayor's acquiescence to each offer of the American barber cannot be branded as entirely stupid. In Japan, as many thousands of Americans well know, the price of a haircut includes a shave and shampoo. And a neck and shoulder massage is invariably given as an extra service to the customer.

The habit of liberal tipping, I am convinced,

117

is mainly because of the inferiority complex of Japanese, especially when they are travelling abroad. Being an extremely self-conscious people and aware that they do not cut a very imposing figure, they hope that they will be able to enhance their prestige by means of extravagant tipping.

The Japanese as a race are fairly homogeneous, but upon closer examination and observation they are found to possess the distinguishing features of several races. Apart from the aboriginal Ainu, who live in the northern island of Hokkaido and whose racial characteristics are distinctly Caucasian, there are many Japanese who are as fair-skinned as Frenchmen or Italians. However, the higher noses and less prominent cheekbones of these peoples are not commonly found in Japan.

On the other hand, there are many dark-skinned Japanese whose features unmistakably resemble those of the South Sea Islanders. There are also others who can easily be taken for Chinese or Korean, and, curiously enough, there are some who seem to have inherited Jewish blood, for they have the typically Semitic prominent nose and swarthy complexion.

Like America, Japan has been the melting pot of many different races who once inhabited the whole great Pacific Basin, and though the Japanese today appear to be extremely homogeneous, they nevertheless exhibit many heterogeneous racial origins.

There is one thing common to all Japanese and that is their jet black hair. I have mentioned that

118

quite a few have skin as fair as a person of Caucasian origin, but even these people invariably have black hair. Human hair color is largely a product of climate. I noticed in northern Scandinavia that the hair of some of the inhabitants is not blond, but almost white, even when they are young. Lack of sunshine is no doubt responsible for this. I remember reading a report by a British doctor who maintained that the eyes of Australian immigrants over many years were gradually becoming narrower and somewhat slanted. While the original Britishers had large eyes, three or four generations in the sunnier climate was enough to make the eyes of their descendants smaller. Similarly, if the Nordic people lived in a more southerly climate for several generations, they would develop darker hair and deeper pigmentation as a protection against the stronger sunshine. The fact that the peoples of southern Europe generally have darker hair and skin bears out this thesis.

We Japanese are all born with a shock of black hair which always remains black, except of course in old age, whereas people in the United States and Europe are born with hair of one color, which almost always changes to another color quite early in life. Another of our distinguishing physical characteristics is the Mongolian spot, which is blue in color and about the size of the ball of the finger. It appears on the spine of babies and disappears at about the age of two years. Besides the Japanese of course, other Oriental babies have this same spot. I have not heard a satisfactory scientific explanation of this marking.

Climatic conditions and diet are largely instrumental in the physical development of any people. Those two factors may not alter one individual's physique, but through several generations they are bound to exert a definite influence and bring about appreciable changes in the physical constitution of any people. My previous observation about the Australians having undergone such a physical evolution is a case in point.

American-born Japanese have, in two generations, already shown an improvement in their physique to the extent that they are now taller, broader, and generally more shapely than their relatives in Japan. Similarly, I know an Englishman who resided for more than twenty years in Japan as a consular officer for his government. Some years ago he went back on leave to England and passed through the United States. I met him in San Francisco. Although he was not Japanese, I was amazed to see the yellowish complexion he had acquired in the course of those two decades' residence in the Far East. I was not the only one who was surprised to see his changed complexion; others also commented on his sallow coloring. The humidity, the quality of the water, and other factors combine to make foreigners appear more and more like the natives of the locality they stay in over the course of years spent there.

Human physical characteristics, therefore, are largely a product of natural surroundings and diet. Insufficiency of dairy products is mainly responsible for the slender bone construction of Japanese and, incidentally, for the deplorable prevalence of tuberculosis. The average Japanese consumes a very small quantity of milk, daily consumption being the infinitesimal amount of 0.02 pints per capita, whereas the corresponding American consumption is about seventy-five times that amount. The number of milch cows in Japan is only about 360,000 head, as against 48,000,000 head in the United States. A shortage of grazing land as well as poor forage for cattle account for this deficiency.

Lack of nourishing food, especially of dairy products, coupled with congested living conditions have given rise to an appalling incidence of respiratory diseases in Japan. Approximately 150,000 people are said to die from tuberculosis each year. The incidence is five times that of the United States and higher than that of most other countries. Altogether it is estimated over a million and a half Japanese are suffering from this deadly disease. Moreover, the critical shortage of hospital space requires that 95 per cent of those stricken be nursed at home, thus increasing the chances of contagion. As it is now, the white plague can be said to be almost a national disease and Japan's No. 1 killer. Although energetic measures are being taken by the Ministry of Welfare to eliminate the disease, a marked improvement in the situation will have to await the achievement of a higher standard of living as well as the awakening of the general public to the menace.

The prevalence of tuberculosis is not a postwar phenomenon; it has been in existence for a number

121

of years. The extreme dampness of the Japanese climate, among other things, contributes to this unfortunate condition. Japanese novels and dramas have always been inclined to tragedy rather than to comedy, and death by tuberculosis is a favorite theme. I may say too that the Japanese conception of a beautiful woman is generally one who is slender and pale. In Japanese drama it turns out more often than not that the person blessed with such beauty is also afflicted with tuberculosis. All audiences can understand the tragic circumstances of such a drama, for the threads of it have often been woven into their own lives.

Japanese legs are not only short but also in many cases not quite straight. This is a result of their habit of squatting on the floor and of mothers carrying their babies strapped on their backs. Another contributing factor is the wearing of *geta,* or wooden clogs, with the "Y" shaped cord or thong, which passes between the big toe and the second toe. In wearing these clogs much power must be concentrated on the toe so that the foot will not slip out while walking and running. Such a continuous exertion develops the muscles of the knee to an extraordinary extent. With daily exercise thus concentrated on development of the knee muscles, there is little opportunity for the development of the rest of the leg. This peculiarity, I think, could easily be corrected by the adoption of Western practices. At present the younger generation use benches and chairs in their schools, which the older generation

122

did not have; rather they sat with their legs tucked under them hour after hour. The result of this change, coupled with the now intensive physical exercise and sports program, is that our limbs are becoming longer and straighter.

The average Japanese hand is sinewy, flexible, and sensitive. Extraordinary dexterity is developed through the use of the brush in calligraphy and by the discipline of many small handicrafts. Intricate and tiny ivory and wood carvings and delicately-painted crockery are ubiquitous in Japan. Such dexterous hands are able to fabricate the tiniest objects with remarkable precision, and to perform the most delicate surgical operation with skill. It is therefore not difficult to understand why in most European countries there is a brisk demand for Japanese chicken-sexers.

The practice of strapping babies upon their mothers' backs is still widespread among the lower classes. This practice contributes to the already large incidence of nearsightedness. Babies perched with their little eyes focussed for long periods of time at such close range are subject to defective eyesight at an early age. Complicated Japanese calligraphy is often blamed for our widespread nearsightedness. The demands of our difficult writing may be partly responsible but that this factor is not the principal one is demonstrated by the fact that the Chinese who use an even more complicated calligraphy than we do have remarkably few cases of nearsightedness. It is my belief that a poor and unbalanced diet with a resulting deficiency of proper vitamins is more responsible for the widespread incidence of poor eyesight than any other factor.

The Japanese habit of squatting or sitting cross-legged for hours at a time develops remarkable strength in the waist. Japanese prowess in swimming is due largely to this fact. Our athletes also distinguish themselves in such events as hopping, jumping, and in marathon races at various international athletic meets, because of this muscular development.

Unlike the Chinese, my countrymen are extremely athletic, and among youth there are virtual addicts to every conceivable sport. The great ambition of many youths today, as in the past, is to participate in the International Olympic Games. Because we are a sensitive people, many of us are moved to tears when some Japanese athlete wins an international event. Perhaps this is another example of our national inferiority complex.

Occasional visits of an American baseball team or swimming team are invariably occasions of nation-wide jubilation. Nowhere else in the world have I seen such enthusiasm for sports evinced by the general public. In fact, in many ways baseball is more popular in Japan than it is in America, its birthplace. I believe that the GI's and other American visitors will agree with this statement. Even such an expensive and exclusive game as golf is played extensively, there being as many as forty-three full-sized golf courses in Japan, and this in a country in which children do not even have enough space for their playgrounds. This shows the extent to which the Japanese will go in order to be able to enjoy this "new-fangled" foreign sport.

Skiing is another sport to which nearly all able-bodied young men and women take a fancy. Even children take to it in great numbers. I have skied in Norway, Switzerland, Russia, and the United States, but nowhere have I seen crowds as huge as in our resorts. The many special trains leaving Tokyo or other big cities for the ski resorts are so packed with skiers that many are forced to stand all night in whatever space they can find. Foreigners are amazed at the enthusiasm displayed by our ski addicts. The zeal and single-mindedness with which the Japanese practice skiing is truly astounding. While at a resort they devote themselves entirely to the sport from early morning until dusk, even skimping on meal hours.

Even though Japanese in their youth are such avid sports fans they virtually cease these athletic activities after they have received their diplomas from schools or colleges. Making their way in the business world forces them to concentrate their attention elsewhere and they devote little time to even the most accessible, although somewhat limited sports facilities. Long working hours prohibit such indulgence. Golf is perhaps the only sport which the well-to-do Japanese man in middle and old age goes in for with any enthusiasm.

Western ballroom dancing is very popular in

125

Japan. However, with our short stature and legs we do not make a very impressive showing on a dance floor, when viewed by Westerners. Great pains are taken to master the intricacies of the various dance steps. Only a bold few would dare to venture in public without having learned at least the rudiments of dancing. As a result of this seriousness, one will not find the hilarity in Japan that is always demonstrated in Western dance halls. The constant self-consciousness and fear that they might make fools of themselves force the Japanese to be absorbed in the steps rather than in the enjoyment of the dance itself. Excellent dancers though many may be, they unfortunately do not always present a graceful picture.

A Japanese friend of mine was very fond of dancing and while abroad danced whenever he had the opportunity. Unfortunately this fellow was extremely short, only about five feet two inches. His legs were, like those of most Japanese, pitifully short. While dancing among a crowd of Westerners he really looked like a dwarf, which fact he was thoroughly conscious of. In his anxiety not to lower the prestige of his countrymen in the eyes of Westerners and at the same time to show his ability as a dancer, he developed an amusing technique. In a dance hall or restaurant as soon as the band started playing, my friend immediately stood up and with his partner stepped boldly to the center of the dance floor, long before the other guests did so. Naturally, he and his partner were stared at curiously by the other people there, but in spite of this he would perform his round of dancing in all solemnity and seriousness. However comical a figure he may have cut, at least he danced with orthodox steps and in perfect time with the music. In this way he used to attract considerable attention and even admiration for his "exhibition dancing." This came to a prompt end, however, the moment the other guests reached the floor. As soon as they started whirling around, he was lost in the crowd. My friend derived considerable satisfaction from his unique dancing methods, which he explained was the only way to compensate for the poor figure his average countryman cut in a Western dance hall!

The Japanese are said to be endowed with weak vocal chords, and for singing Western music their voices are usually small and often discordant. There are few opera singers, especially tenors, who can sing half as well as or in as strong a voice as their Western counterparts. It is also curious that we cannot make the sound of the English letter "L," and hence always "pray" tennis or "herro, prease" on the telephone. Our Chinese neighbors are the other way about and find it difficult to pronounce the letter "R."

The Japanese popular drink is saké, a wine made from rice. It can be compared with sherry. It is not a strong drink, being about 25 proof. However, drunkenness comes quite easily for the Japanese, even with this comparatively mild drink. Most Japanese soon acquire an alcoholic red glow after one

127

glass of beer. And how garrulous some become after but two glasses! We are physically weak with respect to alcohol and show a quick reaction to any intoxicating drink. This is a result of the vegetarian diet to which we have so long been accustomed. The tissues of our stomachs are sensitive to alcoholic beverages. Nevertheless, the Japanese are inordinately fond of saké, which is drunk from a tiny, shallow cup about an inch and a half in diameter. At dinner parties the host and the guests perform a ritual of exchanging cups. The host first offers his cup to the guest and fills it; then the guest drinks its contents. Then the guest dips the other's empty cup into a small bowl of hot water provided at the table, to cleanse it before returning it. Similarly, the guest offers his own cup to the host, who goes through the same ritual. In the course of these interminable exchanges and rounds of saké both the host and guests end up by consuming a considerable quantity of the liquor. The host insists that the guest drink even when the latter has had more than enough. In fact, it is considered impolite not to accept when offered saké. This same custom prevails in both China and Russia, where drinkers indulge in "bottoms up" almost continuously.

At dinner parties it isn't long before the average guest develops a deep red flush and gets quite intoxicated. The Japanese while sober are generally serious and reserved, but when intoxicated they throw off all their reserve and taciturnity and become quite boisterous. They sing, sometimes swear, and become extremely talkative. Most guests at dinner parties —like peoples of other countries throughout the world—drink too much, way beyond their capacity. They become ill and desert the party. Nevertheless, no party is considered a success unless all participants become thoroughly drunk. Personal grudges are often aired, and arguments and quarrels take place. Toward the end of the party, things often become quite wild, and some people may even start dancing stupidly, having lost all sense of decorum. If a party breaks up before all concerned are sufficiently intoxicated, they often move on to another teahouse or tavern for another round. Of course these parties are always stag affairs.

Japanese fondness for such parties is primarily the result of their leading such serious lives in other respects, with so many moral and social restraints. Moreover, there is little occasion for what Westerners call "social gatherings." We are a gregarious people and as individuals are usually forlorn and helpless. We have not learned to enjoy ourselves alone and consequently feel an emptiness when left to ourselves. In Europe or the United States retired men or widows are often seen walking alone in hotel areas or resort towns and they seem quite contented and happy. Such is not the case with us. Unhappiness and mental discomfort are the rule for Japanese when not in the company of others. My countrymen truly enjoy themselves only in the company of other people. By collective drinking at parties, they cast off their self-consciousness and reveal their true selves.

129

In doing business with the Japanese this characteristic must always be borne in mind: one will be disappointed if he expects to talk business with a Japanese in his office. The businessman usually avoids serious conversation with anyone for the first few interviews. It is only after a teahouse drinking party or after a certain amount of intimacy has been achieved that one can pave the way for a real business deal. A business executive, therefore, spends almost every night at some restaurant and conducts his business in the midst of drinking. If obstacles were encountered in a business transaction, they should be overcome at the drinking party. Businessmen are supposed to compromise on a workable arrangement within this alcoholic atmosphere. In my travels I have found that many business executives in other countries also conduct the preliminaries of business at dinners and other social gatherings. But the practice in Japan is deeper and more widespread.

The Japanese are said to be odorless or nearly so, which fact is attributed to frequent bathing. To Japanese, Westerners have a strong body odor which is quite nauseating. This body odor of the average American or European is undoubtedly the result of a heavy meat diet. We find it most curious to read advertisements in Western papers and magazines about lotions and medicines, the use of which will prevent the wrecking of romances and will enhance the user's happiness! The absence of such alluring advertising in Japanese papers or journals is one evidence that the Japanese are comparatively free of body odor. On the other hand, our papers and magazines carry numerous ads of patent medicines and sure-fire remedies for all other mortal ills.

Nevertheless, some Japanese do as a matter of fact have an underarm odor, which is often regarded as a sickness. They even resort to surgery to have the afflicted skin removed. It is a mistake to think that the Japanese are completely free of body odor. A large delegation of Japanese athletes participated in the Olympic Games held in Berlin in 1936. I happened to visit some of them in the locker rooms of the stadium where they had just been participating. Coming in from the events in great perspiration, they were ready to take their showers and dress. I realized at that very moment that the Japanese also have a body odor, an intense one and peculiar to themselves. It is like the odor of fish and pickled radishes combined.

The inside of trains and offices, which are usually poorly ventilated, especially in winter, are permeated with this very same odor. Besides this there is another distinctive odor. Because most Japanese, particularly young men, have coarse hair, the majority use a certain kind of vegetable hair cream to keep their hair in place. The lotion has a peculiar odor so strong as to be downright nauseating to many people. Certainly it is to many foreigners. In crowded places the smell of this hair cream, mixed with the body odor, emits, as the GI's say, "a real aroma."

Human beings, because they are alive, could not possibly be without some odor, and each race, in my opinion, has its own peculiar odor, according to how the people eat and how they live. Travellers in Russia, upon entering one of the major cities, be it Moscow or Vladivostok, cannot but be struck with the peculiar smell—Russian body odor mixed with the all-pervading smell of *mahorka,* the popular Russian tobacco. This peculiar odor permeates literally every nook and corner of the Soviet Union. With the passage of time, a foreigner living there may become accustomed to it, or at least it may not seem to him to be as strong as when he first entered the country.

Some years ago I was coming back from Europe to the Far East via Suez on a French luxury liner. Just a day before the boat pulled into the port of Singapore, there was a slight commotion among the European passengers on board. Off the coast of Singapore, they started smelling what they called *l'odeur de l'extrême Orient,* "the odor of the Far East." They knew then that they were back in the Far East. Still the Frenchmen who made such a fuss over the odor of the Orient are by no means odorless themselves. When I crossed the English Channel into France I could always smell the odor of France, and although it was not repugnant or nauseating, it was a physical reminder that I was in France again. Compared with Occidentals, the Japanese have a low body temperature, a little over 36 degrees Centigrade (96.8 degrees Fahrenheit) being normal. This again may be accounted for by the vegetarian diet, which generates less heat than a meat diet. For us, European waters are too cold even in summer. My countrymen cannot remain long in sea water which Europeans might find quite invigorating. Our swimmers are very particular about the proper season for swimming in the sea. In most parts of the country, they only swim from the middle of July until the end of August. With the beginning of September they stop swimming abruptly, for then the sea becomes quite cool. Few Japanese enjoy swimming unless the water is quite tepid. Of course, swimming in indoor pools is a different story, as these are heated to body temperature.

Some peoples of the Orient, especially in the tropical countries, are extremely precocious. The Japanese, however, are rather slow in maturing and seldom marry at an early age. There is a Confucian teaching to the effect that boys and girls should not sit together after reaching the age of seven years. In prewar years the Japanese followed this exhortation almost to the letter. Hence, coeducation as a system was not practiced in my country. Our houses with their paper screen partitions afford little privacy, but even in this situation, the above training has effectively prevented Japanese adolescents from mixing freely with one another. Also before the war, there was a special subject on all school curricula which taught ethical and moral precepts. One of these was that it is not ethical to indulge in sexual intercourse before one is legally married. Under these circumstances, there was a surprising percentage of young men and women in Japan who preserved their chastity until marriage.

Since the war such moral restraints have largely been removed. Moral laxity among the younger generation has been noticeable. Economic conditions in postwar years have made it extremely difficult for young men to marry before the age of thirty.

However, I must add that I believe that the Japanese are not prone to promiscuity or sexual excess. This also may be one of the effects of a vegetarian diet.

C. Felt

8   Made in Japan

IN prewar years, particularly in the late 'thirties, cheap consumer goods of all sorts made in Japan flooded into world markets. I was greatly surprised to see Japanese toothpaste being sold in a drugstore in Reykjavik, the capital city of Iceland. In Czechoslovakian villages in the remote Carpathian mountains, Japanese celluloid toys were being sold. American and British dime stores were full of trinkets and gadgets which people knew instinctively were of Japanese origin. Americans used to buy our zipper fasteners and the United Kingdom imported butter produced in Hokkaido. A thousand and one items marked "Made in Japan" found their way into every

135

nook and corner of the world, principally because of their cheapness.

The Nagoya and Osaka areas used to hum with commercial activity, and buyers and importers from all over the world went there to purchase Japanese products outright or more frequently to have their own products duplicated. I suppose the world will never know how many millions of tons of goods were produced in Japan and exported, under agreements commencing with "Can you reproduce this article exactly, about 10,000 gross?"

After the world-wide economic depression of the early 'thirties, which began with the stock market crash in 1929, the major industrial countries adopted various measures to stem the tide of Japanese-made goods. These had repercussions which constituted a serious problem for Japan, depending as she did on other lands for most of her raw materials. Likewise, we were dependent on China, India, and the Occident for the major portion of our export markets. Then, as they are today and will be in the future, foreign markets were required for Japanese products in order to sustain the country's rapidly increasing population, which is always ready to burst its bounds.

In the early 'thirties many Japanese believed that the only successful solution to the problem of rising protective tariffs in other countries was for Japan to embark upon a program of colonial expansion in order to secure for herself sources of raw materials as well as foreign markets, both essential for Japan's self-sufficiency and invulnerability as a world power. This argument was advanced mainly by the military and radical elements of the country, but it sounded convincing to many businessmen and intellectual groups. Though many other factors combined to impel Japan to embark on an expansionist program, leading eventually to the Pacific War, there is no denying that this factor of Japan's precarious trading position was fundamental in embroiling the nation in foreign wars of conquest, starting with the invasion of Manchuria in 1931.

Before the war, charges of sweatshop labor and unethical business practices were often levelled against the Japanese people in general and against manufacturers in particular for selling cheaply-priced goods. In fact, Japan was considered a menace to the rest of the world not only militarily but also industrially. Goods produced under such circumstances gained notoriety and in many places were stigmatized as inferior.

Ten years of war and Occupation wrought tremendous changes in Japan's internal situation. Today most of the old sweatshop labor conditions are gone, and workers are strongly unionized. Wages have risen, and working hours are strictly enforced in factories. Of course, owing to the differences in standard of living, great disparities exist among the wage scales of British, American, and Japanese laborers, and these are reflected in the cost of production. It seems to me that such variation in cost is inevitable. As the British worker in many industries is willing to work for less than his American counterpart, so is the Japanese worker willing to work for less than the British. As I look at this issue, it is the question of supply and demand of manpower that is most basic.

Referring to the alleged malpractices of Japanese manufacturers regarding patents, designs, and copyrights, the situation has improved of late. Many manufacturers themselves, especially of textiles and pottery, are keenly interested in protecting their own designs from the pirating of others. Formerly Western industrial skill and mechanical equipment were so far ahead of those in Japan that it was impossible for us to manufacture products which could compete successfully with them. Under these circumstances manufacturers found it easier to turn out imitations of the originals and sell them at very low prices.

In this postwar world countries must buy only from those to which they can expect to sell and also they must be very discriminating, especially when importing. The best markets will not continue to absorb shoddy imitations. While in many respects Japanese industry has lagged behind that of many countries during the past ten years, it has also made remarkable progress in certain fields. Inability to import from abroad created serious problems during the war years. For instance, the war prevented the importation of high-precision ball bearings, which formerly came from the United States, Britain, Germany, and other Western countries. This was a blessing in disguise, because war production, especially in the case of airplanes, required ball bearings as good as imported ones. Necessity is the mother of invention, so the proverb runs, and hence concerted efforts to meet this wartime need led to tremendous improvements not only in this one field of precision ball bearings but also in the field of optical instruments. Today excellent products in both these fields are manufactured for domestic consumption as well as for export. Similar developments took place in the manufacture of cameras. It is strange that the Japanese are skeptical about the quality of their own cameras, for they have too long been under the impression that the Germans made far superior ones. Yet, the fact that such countries as the United States, some South American countries, and Switzerland are buying our cameras is sufficient proof that these products are expertly made and no longer to be classed as cheap imitations.

However, some Japanese products, for example, ships, are not yet up to American and British standards. In shipbuilding, the Japanese are just beginning to adopt electric welding, a technique which our war-enforced isolation kept us from learning. The reasons for some maritime countries placing orders for ocean-going vessels with Japan's dockyards are mainly lower costs and perhaps quicker deliveries. All this does not mean that Japanese manufacturers have stopped imitating foreign goods altogether. Originality in the manufacture of many products is a quality which we unfortunately lack. Almost anything worth copying is imitated. American products above others are most eagerly sought and assiduously copied. Well-known American brands of cosmetics, drinks, candies, and other consumer goods have almost identical products for domestic sale in Japan. Even the format of such periodicals as *Life, Time,* and *Reader's Digest* has been copied by enterprising but unscrupulous publishers.

Cases of infringement of patents and copyrights have, though decreased, not entirely disappeared. Recently, certain soft-drink producers formed a firm by the name of Nippon Cola and tried to imitate Coca Cola. The company used bottles almost identical to those used by the well-known American company. Despite repeated warnings and protests made by the local subsidiary of Coca Cola, Nippon Cola kept right on turning out imitation bottles and did a thriving business. Exasperated by this outright piracy, the Coca Cola representatives finally took the case to court. The court's decision called for the scrapping of 76,000 unsold Nippon Cola bottles in the presence of Coca Cola officials. This drastic punitive measure was meant to be a serious blow to the imitators and was generally thought to have given them a "pause that refreshed" their guilty consciences. On the contrary, the Nippon Cola Company got tremendous publicity as a result of the sensational news of the wholesale scrapping of the bottles. The public conclusion was that Nippon Cola must be an excellent drink, since the Americans were so thoroughly alarmed by Nippon Cola's competitive ability. And so it goes in Japan.

There was one comic incident which fortunately

140

did not lower the estimation of the Japanese in the eyes of customers overseas. Bamboo baskets destined for export were marked "Made in USA." The American customs officials were thoroughly incensed by what they thought was another instance of Japanese imitation and cheating. Upon closer examination, however, it turned out that the baskets were made in Usa, a town in the southern island of Kyushu, and had no connection with America!

The Japanese tendency to almost indiscriminately copy everything Western may be explained by the fact that Japan was for centuries cut off from all contact with scientific progress, which even Occidentals follow with intense interest. All at once a new world was opened to Japan as dramatically as though a theater curtain had been raised. The wonders of mechanical invention dazzled the Japanese just as Americans or Britishers would be dazzled if they were cut off from the rest of the world for half a century and then suddenly have thrust in front of them all that had been accomplished in the meantime.

The Japanese term *hakurai-hin,* meaning literally an article which came by boat, was coined toward the end of the last century. It is popularly used even to this day to denote a foreign-made article of superior quality. Many a merchant has capitalized on this peculiar psychology and has done a thriving business. A British store in Kobe before the war dealt in cheap haberdashery goods, mostly of indigenous manufacture. These items which were wrapped in beautiful paper, were highly valued by

141

many Japanese women because the store was British. At Christmas time, thousands would swarm into this store and proudly carry home packages which they believed to be of British manufacture and therefore superior.

Lately Uncle Sam has grown in stature in the eyes of the Japanese and things American have come to denote, in many cases quite justifiably, articles of superlative quality. Many Japanese in recent years have been cheated when they paid exhorbitant prices for reputable American soap and discovered that what they got was a cake of inferior local make wrapped in the original American wrapping.

Japanese labels and designs on many items produced for export are crude, inartistic, and even gaudy. This, however, should not be so surprising because designs and drawings on articles to be sold abroad have to be of a universal character and therefore "foreign." We are not very good at making foreign designs any more than foreigners are capable of making typical Japanese patterns. On the other hand we are able to create the most exquisite and delicately-colored patterns for our own merchandise. Thousands of American visitors have been impressed by these designs. Wrappings and boxes for Japanese cakes, for example, are extremely artistic and defy imitation. Indigenous ceramics and lacquerware are of such artistic merit and decorative distinction that they are almost unmatched anywhere in the world.

In general the Japanese are at a distinct disadvantage in marketing manufactured goods abroad.

Their inability to design anything original or novel along Western lines forces them to copy whatever is best and most popular on the world market. Therefore, Japanese merchants, except those who handle special items of indigenous design, cannot hope to compete successfully with purveyors of first-rate American and British goods. However, there is a ready market for our goods in other Asiatic countries because of their cheapness and the similarity of taste of the natives to our own. Various patent medicines have for many years enjoyed an almost monopolistic position in Chinese and Southeast Asian markets. Some of the trademarks are as familiar to the Chinese as they are to us. Motor trucks manufactured here are better suited to the bad roads that are found in Korea, Thailand, and other Asiatic countries than are those of superior American make. Manufacturing for this market is something in which the Japanese motor industry can have a monopoly. Racial affinity, together with similarity in standards of living, are the most important factors facilitating the marketing of Japanese-made goods in other Asiatic countries. I was convinced of the validity of this conclusion while observing actual conditions during my extended travels.

Moreover, the newly-independent countries, like India, Pakistan, Ceylon, and Indonesia, all want cheaply-priced consumer goods as well as cheaply-priced capital goods. Japan is in a position to supply a great tonnage of both, whereas America and other Occidental countries are busy supplying other countries with other types of commodities; it is proper that these cater to the needs of the more advanced industrial nations.

Salesmanship is a very important factor in export trade, but the true art has never been known in Japan, nor have we ever been a nation of shop-keepers as are the British or the Chinese. During Japan's feudal period for many centuries commerce and trade were despised as mean occupations. The Japanese are as a rule poor export merchants and are usually outwitted by Chinese and Indians in other parts of Asia. Even in Seoul, the capital of Korea, commercial hegemony was enjoyed by a handful of Chinese merchants even when that country was a part of the Japanese Empire. My countrymen, contrary to the general world opinion, did not have a completely free hand in controlling the economy of Korea.

The only exceptions to this general rule that the Japanese are poor traders are the Osaka merchants, who may perhaps be ranked with Jews and Armenians as the world's smartest traders. Osaka is the second largest city in Japan, with a population of two million, and is situated three hundred and fifty miles west of Tokyo. It is an industrial and commercial metropolis, the greatest in the country. A visitor to that city cannot fail to be impressed with the vigorous vitality that is always displayed there. In Osaka the familiar daily greeting of the inhabitants is: "Are you making money?" This salutation takes the place of "How do you do?" I have heard only one other exception to the universal greeting of "How do you do?" It is the Chinese one of "Have you eaten yet?" In China, where famines are of such frequent occurrence, and where the people are predominantly poor, the rice bowl is something with which everyone is necessarily concerned; hence this greeting. As for the Osaka greeting, it shows that the inhabitants are money-conscious. As a greeting, it has no parallel anywhere else in the world.

The people of Osaka, quite unlike those of the rest of the country, are self-reliant and highly independent. In the Orient, be it China, India, or Japan, government jobs and the government service are a coveted career to which most youth aspire. Osaka people, unique among their fellow Orientals, shun government service, for they aspire to be industrialists, merchants, doctors, and members of other lucrative professions. Being so practical-minded, they do not highly value higher education either.

I happened to spend part of my childhood in Osaka, and I recall from elementary school a classmate of mine who came from a poor family. I had almost forgotten about him when, several years ago, he suddenly turned up in London while I was living there. He called me on the telephone from the swank Savoy Hotel, in which he was occupying an expensive suite with his secretary. He told me that he had gone into the brush manufacturing business as soon as he finished primary school, that he had worked hard to build up his business, and that he was

145

on a business tour of Europe. I likened him to America's Mr. Fuller of Connecticut. He was then in his early thirties but must have already been extremely prosperous. On that pleasant day in London, he did not greet me with the usual "Are you making money?" because he thought, I suppose, that it was not worthwhile to put such a question to me, although most of the conversation did relate to money matters and how he was making effective use of his Jewish agents in the principal cities of Europe. He is typical of the Osaka merchant—self-reliant, practical, and most enterprising.

When another Osaka businessman reached the age of fifty some years ago, he said that he had amassed a fortune of $2,500,000. To commemorate his half century of "profitable life," he decided to do a bit of philanthropic work. One day he went to see the secretary of public education in Tokyo and confided that since he, as a businessman, had devoted himself to money-making and had done not a few ungracious things in the process, he thought in good conscience that it was high time that he do something for the benefit of the community. He then divulged his idea of endowing a woman's college with a grant of $750,000. He sought authorization from the Ministry of Education in Tokyo for the establishment of the endowment. The secretary was moved by the businessman's public spirit and encouraged him to go ahead with his laudable plan.

A few years later the same secretary of the Ministry learned of some trouble in Osaka involving a business college. In due time he called for an investigation. It transpired that the businessman had created the endowment as planned and that the college had been built and was in operation. Now the operation of a private school, if properly managed, is a lucrative business in Japan. The women's college had a large enrollment and was prospering. The businessman-philanthrophist became so interested in the college as a money-making enterprise that he began to regret having made the endowment. However, he decided that he himself should be running the school and therefore tried to oust the trustees and the principal so that he could take over management of the institution; hence the squabble. He had ceased to be the sincere philanthrophist and was now busy making money out of the college. Several years later, at the start of the Pacific War, with typical Osaka astuteness, he sold the college buildings to a munitions factory for the equivalent of $1,120,000!

Just as with tight-fisted Scotchmen and shrewd Jews, many unsavory stories are told of the lives of Osaka merchants. Still there is no denying that they constitute the mainstay of the industrial and business world of Japan. Just why the people of Osaka, unlike the rest of their compatriots, are so commercially minded is interesting. For many centuries Sakai, the port of Osaka, was the center of a flourishing trade with the outside world, notably China. Until the late sixteenth century Osaka was a free city outside the domain of the feudal lords. It was dominated by local merchants. Traders of Osaka had constant

147

dealings with foreign people and became adept at bargaining, and as a result they had their wits sharpened and developed a money consciousness. When Japan started learning Western industrial methods in the latter half of the last century, Osaka was the first section of the country to industrialize. The city soon became known as the "Manchester of the East." It will no doubt emerge again as one of the world's greatest commercial and industrial centers. It may not even be too much to say that this city holds the key to the future of all Japan.

Much has been said of Japan's postwar recovery. The cotton spinning industry has been the first to stage a comeback. Japan had 13,000,000 spindles before the war; all but two million were scrapped during the war. Today's figure is about seven million and this is likely to increase. Textiles comprise about half our exports, totaling $460,000,000 annually. Machinery makes up less than one-sixth of our export total, or approximately $190,000,000. These figures are for the year 1953. Sewing machines accounted for $20,000,000 and bicycles for $7,000,000. Other items included cameras, binoculars, watches and clocks, ball bearings, clinical thermometers, rolling stock, Diesel engines, ships, three-wheeled motorcycles, trucks, and toys. Japanese steel production, which was about nine million tons per year at its peak during the war and some five million in the year 1935, is now over six and one-half million tons. Some indication of Japanese economic recovery may be seen in the fact that in 53 the country's total exports amounted to $1,200,000,000, whereas prewar exports averaged a half billion dollars. Even allowing for depreciation of dollar value during the last ten years, export trade has staged a remarkable comeback in the last few years.

One reason, other than the generous American economic aid, that Japanese industries have revived so rapidly and exports increased is that after many years of wartime dislocation, the world had need for many consumer goods. It is just like parched land absorbing rain after a long spell of dry weather. The future of Japanese foreign trade, therefore, is not as rosy as it seems today. Despite recent recovery, the Japanese economy is still in a highly precarious position. Unless Japan succeeds in vastly increasing her industrial production and foreign trade, the future of the country is indeed gloomy. Japan's future thus depends on many factors, some of which are quite beyond her control.

Japan has always to contend with the problem of overpopulation. Already, sixteen million people have to be fed with imported food. Japan has eleven million more people today than at the time of the surrender in 1945. Moreover, the natural population increase per year is 1,500,000. The economic drag of an impoverished mass plus the additional burden created by a rapidly expanding population cannot be made light of. In these days of mass production and increased mechanization, surplus manpower tends to become more and more of a liability.

No manufacturing country was ever so deficient

149

in raw materials as Japan is. Even in prewar years Japan never produced more than a third of its iron ore requirements. Almost all important raw materials have to be imported. Today with a large part of Asia under Communist rule or control, access to raw materials has become exceedingly difficult. It is difficult to say whether this situation will improve or worsen in the future.

Dissolution of the zaibatsu, or big monopolistic industrial combines, such as Mitsui or Mitsubishi, has been a severe blow to the Japanese economy. Just as the average Japanese working as an individual in government is "feeble and inefficient," so is the individual merchant, with the possible exception of the people of Osaka. The zaibatsu, economic empires which branched out in all directions and formed a maze of interlocking cartels and combines, had no parallel in the annals of modern commercial history. The Chinese are smart businessmen when their acumen operates within the bounds of their family circles. But when they incorporate into a joint stock company, their energies seem to degenerate into fighting among themselves and therefore cannot be put to effective use in the markets of the world. On the other hand, the Japanese businessman is at his best when working in concert with his associates.

Joint stock companies in Japan were run on a paternalistic basis and to the mutual advantage of all concerned. In prewar years the ambition of many a college graduate was to get a job with Mitsui, Mitsubishi, or some other zaibatsu combine of great prestige. Employees of these organizations were happy and contented, since in general their positions were secure. This factor of security ranks high in a Japanese' total ambitions, which as a rule are rather modest. The zaibatsu system, utilizing to a maximum extent Japanese group acumen, made possible the accumulation of tremendous capital and with its world-wide ramifications was ideally suited to large-scale development of foreign trade.

The trading firms which exist today are petty in size and not strong enough to compete on world markets. They are at a distinct disadvantage in expanding foreign trade. There is, however, a definite tendency for those dissolved zaibatsu groups to amalgamate again into larger organizations; the Mitsubishi Trading Company has been formed, with the prewar organization as its nucleus. Nevertheless, it will still be many years before this company will be half as powerful as it was before the war.

West from Osaka across the vast Eurasian continent and right to the shores of western Europe, there is not one single industrial center worthy of the name. Modest as the prewar scale of Japan's industrial power was, she will have to go far to attain her previous position as the workshop of Asia, and to turn out all the goods required by Asia's teeming millions. Furthermore, the Japanese economy of the postwar world is, I believe, so closely linked with that of America that Japan is already part and parcel of the American economic sphere. American and Japanese economies are complimentary in many respects. The latter is in a position to supply the needs of Asia, while the highly advanced American economy can fulfill the needs of the more advanced countries. In short, Japan is destined to play the role of a junior partner in the American economy. This close economic interdependence is a logical condition while the Asiatic continent is menaced by communism.

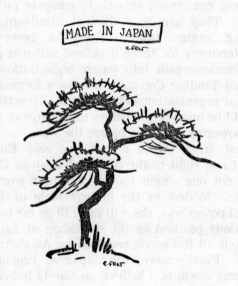

9   WPA for 88 Million People

GEOGRAPHICALLY, Japan is composed of several thousand islands, only four of which are by themselves as large as the state of Connecticut; the others are so small that they are not of great importance. The total area of the country is about the same as that of California, but the percentage of arable land is much less. One-third of the area of California is under cultivation while the cultivated area of Japan is only one-eighth of the total area. The larger part of the country will always be untilled, for it consists of mountains and hills. Although beautiful to look at, they are not productive. While it is difficult for people to appreciate this land shortage, I have talked with many Americans who have travelled throughout the country, and they always express admiration for the tremendous energies expended on carving fields out of the sides of mountains, giving us extra if only marginal areas of cultivation.

Even mountainous Switzerland contains six times more agricultural land proportionately than Japan, where the total area under cultivation is 20,000 square miles. A population of 88,000,000 people must subsist on the produce of this area, supplemented by food purchased from abroad and by fish and seaweed obtained from the neighboring waters.

Overpopulation is apparent everywhere in Japan. Even in rural localities children are often seen playing on the highways, roads, and lanes—unmindful of the traffic hazard, which has grown with the years and taken its toll. Their natural energies force them to play in such places simply for want of open spaces, not to mention regular playgrounds. In the side streets of urban areas, great numbers of young men can frequently be seen practicing baseball, their favorite game, to the real annoyance of the pedestrians, motorists, and cyclists. Naturally, Japanese children, like children of other countries, would rather play in the safety of a playground, but many of them are denied such a luxury. Generations have grown up without proper space to play in.

A European diplomat who was stationed in Tokyo some years ago was an avid swimmer. He was particularly fond of jumping in the water without any clothes on whenever the opportunity presented itself. He constantly looked for secluded coves along the wooded seacoast. He told me that many times he came across a suitable place which he thought was miles from nowhere, but no sooner had he started splashing about than out of the clear blue sky would emerge a swarm of curious children to watch him, amazed at his antics. It was his final opinion that along the entire seacoast there was no place one could bathe without encountering other human beings within a matter of minutes.

In Kagoshima, the southernmost prefecture of the country, there are several villages located along the mountainous peninsula on a narrow strip of land barely wide enough for a house of an average family of ten people. The inhabitants engage in small-scale coastal fishing and in tilling the tiny strips of land around their houses. Because the soil is of recent volcanic origin, it is too poor for growing rice. So the people grow sweet potatoes as their staple food. Peanuts are about the only other item that can be grown in that soil. The climate there is equable, and I saw swarms of children running barefooted in the streets in winter.

I went to see the youthful mayor of the principal town in the district, who was a university graduate and a person who could be called an intellectual. Thoroughly alarmed at the extraordinary fertility, not of the soil, but of the human beings in that particular locality, the first thing that I talked to the mayor about was the possibility of actively introducing birth control among the villagers. I discovered much to my disappointment that the mayor himself had eight children. Recently I learned that in that interesting locality three hundred and fifty young men had applied for three vacancies in the local constabulary. Selection under such difficult circumstances is disheartening, as even those without personal experience will realize.

In densely-populated Japan there is no land which can be called valueless. Much ordinary farm land sells for the equivalent of $3,000 an acre, although this measurement is rarely used in calculating land area. In the larger urban areas the price of land is utterly exhorbitant. There is a saying in Japan to the effect that "a lump of soil is equal to a lump of gold." This is a most appropriate expression in referring to a choice urban lot in the heart of a business district. Land is sold in terms of a small area, the *tsubo,* six feet by six feet. In first-class residential areas of Tokyo this tiny piece of land will cost as much as $150. One needs at least two hundred of these units to accomodate a small house. Thus the land alone would cost $30,000, and even this would be too small to build a garage in addition to the house. House and land in Japan do not necessarily go together, and one can build a house and own it on somebody else's ground. This is a common practice. The owner of the house is protected by law and is not subject to the vagaries of the land owner once he has built a house on the other's lot. He cannot be evicted as long as he pays the rent regularly under stipulated conditions.

Farms in Japan are naturally very small, averaging less than two acres. This figure includes upland pastures and plains, which constitute fully one-third of what is counted as cultivated area. What a tremendous contrast with this can be seen in the United States. My companions and I stared out speeding train windows in deep silence at the vast expanses of land that we saw either being planted, or in pasture, or yielding their harvests. We thoughtfully considered our own country's lands, small and overpopulated. It has often been pointed out that the population of this country is not as dense as Belgium or England. But the land of these countries is almost wholly arable, and therefore conditions are completely different from mountainous Japan. There is more good farm land in mountainous Kentucky than there is in all of Japan, as we discovered in amazement on our tour of the United States.

In some parts of the country the soil is fairly fertile, but in others it is so thin and old that, coupled with undependable climatic conditions, crops are uncertain. It is only through intensive use of fertilizers that the soil of Japan is made at all productive. Rotation of crops is a luxury which never can be practiced by our farmers, in contrast to standard procedure in the West.

Tiny patches of land are called farms in Japan and are cultivated with the utmost care. In America their nearest counterparts would be flower gardens. The plants are coddled and nursed to maturity with an attention to detail which American or Canadian farmers would never conceive of. Rice or wheat is planted in nursery beds as are lettuce and tomatoes in America. When the young plants have attained sufficient strength, they are very carefully transplanted to the paddy field, from which every weed has been carefully removed. Thereafter the cultivation of each plant is a daily task to which as much care is given as an expert American florist would bestow upon his favorite rosebush. Every insect is picked off and any weeds appearing are pulled out before they sap the fertility of the weary soil. If a farmer cannot nurse a weak plant back to vigor, he immediately replaces it with another from the nursery bed, because not a square inch of the tiny fields must be unproductive at the time of harvest.

Thus, intensive agriculture absorbs the energies of forty per cent of our total population. The percentage was down to about thirty-five per cent immediately before the war, but with the influx of millions of repatriates and displaced persons from overseas, the figure is much higher at present. I am told by many that the agrarian population has now reached the saturation point.

With such intensive cultivation in which a great deal of manual labor is applied, we are able to produce about eighty per cent of our total staple food requirements. Introduction of farming equipment and machinery by "modernists" has long been advocated, but little progress can be noted, and the farmers go on using their native implements. In order to keep so many millions employed in farming there is perhaps no other alternative. Overpopulation and the vast number of tiny independently-owned farms throughout the country are both causes for as well as effects of the use of native farming methods. This vicious circle is, I believe, unique to Japan.

The meagerness of the soil has always made the struggle for existence hard in Japan. Scarcity in almost all respects has profoundly affected the national life and character of the people. Just imagine what the struggle for existence in the United States would be if the entire population were jammed into the state of Texas. Even the many Texans who proudly tell of the greatness of their empire would feel the pressure on their 8,000,000 people if 141,000,000 more eager persons crowded around them. A natural result of this extreme congestion is callousness toward human life. One of my companions who recently visited the United States remarked that one of the things which impressed him most strongly was that pedestrians had the right of way. In China and Japan automobiles and trucks generally go about at full speed honking their horns and dispersing unlucky pedestrians who happen to be in the way. Crowds "give," as the GI's say, but I should add that many are caught in the giving.

First-aid kits also are things seldom found in places where Westerners are used to seeing them. Recently I went skiing at one of the most popular mountain resorts in northwestern Japan. At the *yadoya,* or inn, where I stayed, there was no equipment for first aid, not even a small bundle of bandages. I shuddered to think what would happen if a skier came back bleeding from a bad accident. Medical aid comes from a neighboring town several miles away. A doctor has to be sent for in emergencies and that is apparently the only solution.

From the point of view of Westerners, another example of callousness toward life is the absence of fire escapes in big buildings and hotels, which are not provided for by Japanese architects. Escape from fires is accomplished, if at all, by the use of canvas shoots from windows, more suitable for children than for adults. Overcrowding of vehicles and watercraft is common. Recently in one of the canals which crisscrosses Yokohama, a barge used as a hostelry for day laborers turned over, and many casualties resulted. The barge had room for only forty persons, but as many as two hundred and sixty-four had been packed into it. This is an extreme case, but such "careless" overcrowding and lack of necessary safety measures have been responsible for many tragedies.

Throughout Japan, in big factories or small shops, offices or banks, there are great surpluses of employees. A maddening ritual takes place whenever one transacts even the most trivial business. One needs only to keep an account with a Japanese bank to get a forcible illustration of this. Painfully often I have watched the way a bank's unoiled machinery works in Japan. I have watched the same procedures in New York, London, Geneva, and many other cities of the world. On some occasions in Japan it has taken as long as thirty minutes after a check and bank book were presented at the teller's window before the cash was actually received.

Elsewhere, the cashing of a check in a bank takes but a simple thirty seconds.

Precautions in Japanese banks are sometimes carried to the point of absurdity. What is done is that the teller stamps the check with his seal and passes it back to a bookkeeper who checks the pass-book with the ledger to see that the entries tally. A second bookkeeper enters the new check on both books and passes both of them to the chief cashier, who examines all the entries to see that they are correct and then endorses an order for the payment of the money. A fifth clerk records the endorsement and makes a final check. The documents then go to a sixth man, who, if there has been no hitch in the proceedings and you are still waiting, pays the money. Thus six men who take care of the cashing of one check would not be able to take care of one-sixth the number of patrons handled by Western banks.

I had such exasperating experiences with ordinary banks that I decided a couple of years ago to patronize one which had been active in foreign exchange in prewar years and whose staff had some foreign training. My hope was to get speedier service. I was rudely betrayed in this expectation, for here too the process took, on an average, fifteen to twenty minutes. Being disgusted one day I told the teller and chief cashier that I was an extremely busy man and could not possibly wait during these repeated twenty-minute periods just to cash a check or deposit some money. Whenever I have come

161

since then, everyone behind the counters murmurs and whispers about my arrival, and they all try to dispose of my business in rapid time—ten minutes! I am afraid that I am a most disliked customer for demanding such top priority service. Other customers seem to wait their twenty minutes and say nothing about it.

Likewise, most governmental offices are extremely overstaffed, and efficiency suffers as a result. I know a departmental chief in the Tokyo Metropolitan Office who, being of high rank, occupies a large room, which he shares with one clerk and two tea-serving girls. One of the latter would surely be thrown out of a job in the event that an American electric water dispenser were installed. As for the other, I can see little earthly reason for her presence except perhaps to answer occasional telephone calls. Whenever I call on this friend, I see these two girls either leisurely sipping tea or languidly reading the office newspapers.

In the United States, my companions and I noticed that state governors usually had one or two personal secretaries and perhaps a clerk. In Japan, a prefectural governor will have six such private secretaries and clerks, all of whom will be crowded into an adjoining room and have the work to do that a staff half their number in the United States would do.

Some years ago I had to go see a prefectural governor on business. I went to the capital city by train and was met by a couple of junior officials from the governor's office. Looking around the station, they asked me if I had come alone. At the time I did not quite understand the question, but I later found out that it was unthinkable for me, as a governmental official of some rank, to come there to visit the governor unaccompanied by junior officials. As I alighted from the train carrying my own suitcase, these two prefectural officials vied with each other to snatch it and carry it for me. To them it was equally unthinkable that a national official from Tokyo would carry his own bag. They thought such behavior beneath the dignity of a governmental official.

Japanese railroad stations are often over-crowded not only with prospective passengers but also with great numbers of people who have come to see their friends off. If a person is going away from his locality for any length of time, he is usually surrounded by scores of relatives and friends. Business and governmental offices become empty as staff members go to the station. Neither the government nor commercial employers seem to mind these frequent absences, the reason being, I suppose, that most of them do not have too much to do anyway. Even if they are employed, they are, as it were, only partially employed, and they can be absent from their offices with relative impunity. This congregating in the stations could not take place in the United States.

In 1942 I boarded a Swedish liner from New York bound for Portuguese East Africa, where I was to transship to a Japanese steamer to go back to Japan. Because of war conditions, both Swedish and Japanese ships were used for repatriation, and they were crowded to capacity with returning passengers. On the Swedish ship at mealtime one steward took care of two tables with a total of eight passengers and did an admirable job. When I changed ships at Lorenço Marques in East Africa, I was very surprised to find two Japanese stewards serving a table of six, and at times the service was maddeningly slow. It was already the second year of the war, but Japan still had an abundant supply of manpower.

The great newspaper *Asahi,* an influential eight-paged daily, has more than six thousand people on its payroll. Japanese newspapers, especially those of the *Asahi*'s standard, have wonderfully-edited columns with full coverage of world news, something demanded by millions of subscribers. Yet there is no earthly need for so many employees. What a heyday a good personnel efficiency expert would have in showing how much increased productivity per person could mean in savings to these papers!

Japanese hotels generally maintain three times the number of service people that American hotels do. I should say that inns have still larger proportions. As soon as a guest arrives at a Japanese inn and is shown to his room by a hall porter, immediately a maid shows up to assist him in undressing. It is an old custom for a guest at an inn either to take a hot bath upon arrival or to change into a kimono in order to relax. Even if she does not actually assist in undressing, the maid will stand by while you undress and take each garment, including your underwear. All of these are hung in the proper place and those needing it are taken to be pressed. In the meantime another maid will turn up with hot green tea. Thus you will be waited on by several maids, one after the other, almost continuously during your stay at the inn. As a result, there is practically no privacy in a Japanese hotel, particularly in comparison with hotels in the United States or Europe.

I have pointed out that the superabundance of employees in business and industry adversely affects efficiency. The same work is done by several persons. It could be handled more efficiently by one or two persons rather than three or four. Thus everyone "takes it easy" and rarely seems to hustle. A visit to a Japanese office is enough to convince anyone of this.

Even in a small office all employees, except section and department heads, are seated in rows, like soldiers in a mess hall. Although each is given his own work space, desks are all pushed together in double rows so that one person is seated next to another and also facing another. This jamming is a result of lack of space due to overstaffing of the office. This seating arrangement is conducive to gossiping and chatting, which as a matter of fact many employees indulge in. To make matters worse, visitors are always shown into the office, even if on personal business. Countless hours are spent

165

chatting with friends and fellow workers. No one can avoid hearing the conversations, and everyone is distracted. It is well-nigh impossible to concentrate on one's work under such circumstances.

Office hours are not rigidly observed. Even if employees come in late in the morning, it is generally condoned. Since the end of the war, tardiness has become the norm. In most offices employees are required to sign an attendance sheet, which is collected at a certain hour. This method is not an effective means of checking attendance. The stamping of one's seal on a paper or document takes the place of a signature in Japan. In any large organization a person can delegate another to stamp with his seal and then show up later with impunity. Incidentally, I should explain further that one never signs a bank check or document by hand in Japan. Instead, everyone has a *han,* or seal, which is made to order and sometimes registered with the local government office of the individual's residence. It is used everywhere and on every occasion when an official signature is required.

When the day's work is over, office workers often do not seem to be in a particular hurry to leave. They may stay on and indulge in conversation or gossip or even play games. A friend of mine, after having been employed in various Japanese business offices, recently joined a reputable French firm in the city of Kobe. The salary which he receives is no more than what he had been getting before. Yet he was agreeably surprised to find tidiness, order, and punctuality reigning in his new office. Seats and desks were arranged more like those of a classroom. Each person had his own desk, and all faced the same direction, so that each employee could concentrate on his work without interference from his fellow workers. At five o'clock in the afternoon he was happy to find that he could leave his office on time, whereas in his former job he had to stay on in the office even though he had nothing to do except wait until his superiors left. My friend told me that he never wanted to go back to another Japanese firm, even though he might receive higher wages. His case, however, is a little exceptional, for most Japanese do not like exacting punctuality.

This factor of punctuality has never been ingrained on the Japanese mind. Except in Tokyo and other large cities, meetings are usually held long after the scheduled times, but those attending them do not particularly mind this, nor do they protest. I have always made it a point to show up at meetings at the appointed times, but usually there are so few at the meeting places that I sometimes wonder if I haven't come by mistake to the wrong place or on the wrong date. After a while, however, people start coming, but it is often a full half hour before the meeting is opened. This is particularly the case with dinner parties. The punctuality as practiced in the West of arriving at the host's home within a few minutes of the appointed time is not known in Japan. The Japanese do not like to be hurried.

Oriental peoples as a rule are indifferent to

167

being on time. Beside the Japanese, I should add that the Chinese and Russians are notorious for their slowness and lack of punctuality. When I went to Moscow, I heard the word *sichas* quite soon and learned that it means "at once." The Russians often use it when urging someone to do something quickly. Yet in actual practice *sichas* means anything from forty minutes to one hour. American residents and GI's in Japan learned only too promptly our *hayaku,* or "hurry up." I must add that it calls for a shorter length of time than the equivalent Russian expression.

Returning to the subject of office workers, I should like to add that the Japanese are not in any particular hurry to leave the office, since they have nothing much else to do. Most of the offices have some sort of heating in winter, and the workers can keep warm as long as they stay there. When they go home, as I have pointed out before, they get chilled, for their houses are devoid of heat. Therefore, they say to themselves, "Why should I go home and be uncomfortable?" Also the after-hours gatherings always furnish gossip, discussion, and jokes.

After the end of the war the Labor Standards Law was enacted, mainly at the instance of the Occupation authorities. Employees are now paid overtime for work performed after office hours. In itself the new labor law is admirable, but it has no *raison-d'être* in Japan. The manner in which the Japanese carry on work during stipulated office hours, sipping tea, gossiping, and reading newspapers, does not justify this luxurious practice of the West. In fact, since the law came into effect, there have been many Japanese who try to while away more time during office hours and then start to work seriously after closing time, in order to get a little overtime pay.

Although office workers seem to idle away their time doing almost nothing, they have to be careful lest they lose their jobs. In other words they have to make themselves useful in one way or another, and this often takes the form of insinuating themselves into the good graces of their superiors. For this reason very few government officials or office employees ever take prolonged vacations. By law they are entitled to three weeks' holiday during each year. However, very few avail themselves of this opportunity, because they are apprehensive lest while on vacation their places be filled by people who might try to learn the work so well that by the time they return they might lose their jobs, because their usefulness had been severely questioned.

Similarly, officials, especially those of lesser rank, try to keep all important files to themselves and seldom allow others to have access to them. This tactic is obvious. When one man has to remain away from the office because of illness, for example, he locks up his files. The result is that when his superior wants to find out about a certain matter relating to his work, no one else can give a satisfactory answer. The superior naturally misses the absent one, and his importance is enhanced. This

169

artful bureaucratic behavior is conscientiously employed. I realize that the Japanese are not the only ones familiar with this ruse, for I have heard some of my foreign friends decry similar tendencies among their own people.

All of these petty practices—and some are even evil—are brought about by a surplus of employees, but no organization can drastically streamline its staff, for fear of giving rise to social unrest. It is my impression that government offices, with a few exceptions, could cut down on their personnel by one-fourth, and thereby increase efficiency. Even profit-conscious business establishments maintain staffs substantially larger than are actually required. Through the use of labor-saving office equipment, perhaps one-fourth of the present number of personnel would suffice quite well.

Since everyone has to be employed in some way or another in order to make a living, employees have to quit their jobs at around the age of forty-five years or at the most fifty. A government employee, for example, usually reaches the top of the hierarchy at about forty years and then is forced to resign in order to "make room for those who come in his footsteps." This expression is current and is customarily used when retiring from service. It is well-nigh impossible to remain in the organization much beyond that age because there are so many young aspirants, who will eventually squeeze in. After retirement, he has to seek some odd job elsewhere. He may become an advisor to some group or institution, usually in a capacity related to his previous position. This is usually a sinecure, which is barely enough to sustain himself for the several years that he has yet to live.

The struggle for existence is so severe that the Japanese will often stoop to running down other people, even the closest of friends. An official who works and strives in a government agency, for instance, may even go so far as to find fault with any of his colleagues who may be in his way. An accusation or rumor may be circulated which can result in a rival getting into trouble, even in some cases being fired. Although such an accusation may be completely fabricated, the method can be justified in the eyes of the Japanese. The Military Government Teams in the various prefectures during the Occupation used to receive numerous anonymous tips about all sorts of people. They were written with the sinister intent of having the person mentioned get into trouble with the Occupation authorities. Petty personal gossip involving mutual friends is a part of daily conversation and with many a favored topic.

Internal strife always characterized Japanese life in our overseas colonies and actually thwarted the program of expansion. Whenever a person achieved a certain measure of success through dint of sheer effort he soon became the target of willful calumny and intrigue by his compatriots with the specific object of undermining his position. His jealous rivals would take immense delight in eliminating him from his share of activity, not giving much thought to the time when they too would be liquidated by a similar process. This sort of activity is typical not only in Japan but also in many parts of the world where the Japanese have emigrated in large numbers. Cooperation and mutual assistance are seldom practiced among them. When any mutual assistance does take place, it is often either spurious or short-lived. However, perhaps I am being overly severe in this matter.

Among first-generation Japanese in California there are separate associations according to the prefecture from which they originally came. Provincialism and narrow-mindedness thus characterize their social life. There are Japanese associations in many places, but instead of being welfare or mutual-aid groups, they are hotbeds of intrigue and strife among the various bosses. These associations in North America, not to mention others in Central and South America, which can often claim large memberships, do more harm than good to their members. They impede rather than promote their interests and welfare. I know successful businessmen in California who have kept aloof from such organizations and shun them as much as possible; one man confided that this was the only way of achieving success abroad. While travelling in French Indo-China, I met a real go-getter businessman who did his business with a British bank. He did not like to patronize the Japanese banks, for he said that there his financial condition often leaked out to others and was used to his disadvantage.

Perennial overpopulation has not only made life miserable for millions but also has given rise to many undesirable characteristics which have become virtually national. A high ranking American official who had spent several years in military government in various parts of the country during the Occupation and who was a remarkably keen observer, told me that Japan would indeed be a happy country if its population could be stabilized at about 40,000,000, and I heartily agreed. What does the future hold for Japan in this important regard? Will we be able to cope somehow with this problem, as serious as it is?

10   Earthquake, Thunder, Fire, and Father

FROM time immemorial, earthquake, thunder, fire, and father have been called the four major terrors in Japanese life. That a father is singled out as one of the major terrors, however, needs some explanation.

In Japan the average "dad" is regarded as a disciplinarian strong enough to awe children into obedience. The father is the master of the household and wields dictatorial powers in all its affairs. Filial devotion and absolute obedience of children to their parents are the two virtues which have long

175

been preached as the cardinal principles of our family system. The sternness of mothers, however, is often tempered by mercy, but fathers stand out as strict disciplinarians. An unruly Japanese child is often lulled into obedience the moment he is told that his father is coming. Such strict family discipline, however, is no longer general, except in old-fashioned and rural homes.

Denied an abundance of fertile soil, the Japanese are even denied safe possession of the small areas of land they do occupy. Typhoons, floods, earthquakes, and volcanic eruptions—all the hysteria of Mother Nature which are most terrifying to mankind and most destructive of his possessions—are in Japan not isolated incidents experienced once in ten years; they are tragic events to be expected every year, just like the coming of frost in winter or the heat in summer. The many rivers, which in gentler moods flow in graceful curves through beautiful green valleys, become raging torrents with each rainy season, devastating wide areas in their paths. Most of the mountains which crown my country with truly majestic beauty are of volcanic origin, and some which have long been considered extinct suddenly become dangerously active and force the evacuation of large areas which for centuries have been occupied by farms and villages.

In the mountains some one hundred and twenty miles north of Tokyo nestles Karuizawa, a famous summer resort for foreign residents. It was there that most of the diplomatic corps in Tokyo took refuge during the war to avoid the incessant bombings. Immediately behind the town of Karuizawa is Mt. Asama, which erupts now and then, covering a large area with fiery ashes and making many hundreds of inhabitants homeless. Foreigners, however, after living in Japan for some time, seem to become indifferent to the danger or at least to assume a fatalistic attitude toward volcanic eruptions, for they still congregate around Karuizawa. It is a precarious spot, at the mercy of the frequent wrath of nature. About fifty volcanoes are still considered active, and there have been few decades in recent history without a destructive eruption of one or more of them.

Earthquakes visit Japan with great frequency and terrorize everyone. Earthquakes are something to which no one ever really becomes accustomed. One may get used to tossing about in a severe storm on the high seas and may even become immune to seasickness, but when the solid earth begins to rock and quiver, the stoutest hearts grow faint. In Japan, this natural fear is heightened by a knowledge of Japanese history, which contains a tragic record of numerous earthquakes bringing death and destruction in their wake.

In ancient times the Japanese believed that a huge catfish lay under the ground, and every tremor of the earth was attributed to the movements of this monster fish. The first earthquake recorded in Japanese history is supposed to have taken place in 286 B.C. Tradition has it that it was during this first

177

earthquake that Mt. Fuji and Lake Biwa, the highest mountain in Japan and the largest lake, each appeared simultaneously. Since then numerous major earthquakes have been recorded throughout Japanese history, at intervals of some thirty or forty years. No part of Japan, with the possible exception of the northern island of Hokkaido, has been immune from these devastating visitations of nature.

Two minutes before noon on the first of September, 1923, the Tokyo-Yokohama area was rocked by a severe quake. Many wooden buildings tumbled in ruins in a few seconds, and kitchen fires which had been kindled to prepare the noonday meal instead lit fire to all inflammable materials, and in a matter of a few minutes a great part of Tokyo, a city at that time of five million inhabitants, was in flames. By the time the residents realized their peril, the wind had whipped hundreds of small fires into great walls of flame, which began to envelop streets, fire breaks, and canal areas at terrific speed.

Frantically the panic-stricken people seized what belongings they could and began to flee, some towards Tokyo Bay, some to vacant lots, parks, school playgrounds, toward higher ground, to canals, ponds, and rivers. The flames, riding the gale, moved faster and faster. The refugees dropped their bundles and ran on; the crowds of panting, gasping, choking men, women, and children became thicker and thicker in every open space—in the broad avenues and in the winding, narrow alleyways of old Tokyo.

The people ran blindly from the searing flames

178

only to come to a gasping milling halt before new barricades of fire thrown up by the treacherously shifting wind. Some stopped to gauge the direction of the wind, but no sooner had they determined a new way to safety than the wind changed its course again to cut off their line of escape. The escape rapidly became a wild stampede, and the old, as well as the very young, the lame, and the sick, were the first to go down beneath trampling feet. They lay where they fell, and the fortunate ones were those who died before the flames reached them.

Many ran for blocks to reach one of the bridges that provided an exit from the burning area, only to find that the bridge had been destroyed. They leapt frantically into the water to escape from the searing heat and thousands were drowned. The flames roared on gulping up great draughts of oxygen causing other thousands to die in shelters, in the streets, and in the canals, like so many fish left gasping on the bottom of a lake that has been drained dry. Altogether, 150,000 persons perished in the infernal conflagration, which raged for three days and nights, almost completely destroying the cities of Tokyo and Yokohama.

Japanese houses are built mainly of wood, principally because of its easy availability. Stone or brick buildings are extremely dangerous in earthquakes. Wooden frame buildings have much more strength and flexibility in resisting seismic shocks than structures of stone or brick. If care is taken in its construction, a building of wooden structure

179

will successfully withstand an earthquake of extreme severity. Though some of the old buildings in Japan have been destroyed by quakes due to defects in construction, there have been some remarkable examples, such as the five-story pagodas of Buddhist temples with their seemingly unstable architecture, which have successfully withstood severe earthquakes for centuries.

Since the great earthquake disaster of 1923, the Japanese have made intensive studies of earthquake-proof construction. It has been found that a reinforced steel and concrete building of eight to ten stories can withstand earthquakes remarkably well. Besides wooden dwellings, reinforced concrete buildings are now the mainstay of our architecture.

Of all the natural calamities that befall the hapless islands of Japan, nothing comes with more clocklike regularity than the typhoons. Our Japanese calendar gives two dates for them—the 210th and 220th day. These dates are computed from the beginning of the lunar year, and the first usually falls within the first few days of September. It is then that violent typhoons originating in the South Seas sweep up to the Japanese archipelago with tremendous fury and after bombarding some part of the country sweep off into the northern waters. Each year some part of the country comes within the path of a typhoon and is devastated by torrential rains and ferocious winds, with vast damage in both life and property. Not content with one major attack, Nature ordains that Japan shall be visited by another, usually of less intensity, on the 220th day, which gives a finishing touch to the already devastated area.

The route of these annual typhoons deviates slightly from year to year so that one year it may strike the Tokyo-Yokohama area, while the Osaka-Kobe district may be the target the next year. In any event, no part of the country can completely escape these annual visitations. The disaster is felt most strongly by the rice farmers, for this crop starts maturing just about that time of year.

The typhoon usually brings with it a deluge of water, flooding rivers and valleys. Thousands of acres of farmland and tens of thousands of inhabitants are washed away overnight. People in the stricken area, homeless, landless, and penniless, float on tiny rafts and boats on inundated lands for days on end until the fury finally subsides.

After the deluge the people set to work again, starting from scratch, pumping out water, clearing the land, sowing seeds for emergency crops, and building wooden shacks to live in. A great deal could be done in the way of flood prevention by building better dams and stronger river embankments and diverting river water into regular channels. But the government never has sufficient funds to provide for such long-range programs, even though officials may have millions of yen to spend on banquets and other meaningless activities. The voice of the people is either too weak or not listened to. After a major disaster the stricken inhabitants seldom clamor for flood-prevention measures; rather they meekly set

181

to work again, exposing themselves to repetition of such disasters year after year.

Numerous fires, big and small, occur during the winter months in Japan. Tokyo, the capital city, is particularly notorious for the number of fires there each winter. "Blossom of Yedo" was the nickname given to the capital city of Japan for many centuries because of the numerous fires which lit up the city like red flowers blossoming. Yedo was the name of Tokyo before 1868, the year of restoration of imperial rule. Then, as now, Japanese houses of wood and paper were easy prey for the flames. Also, Tokyo in winter months is subject to extremely strong, northerly winds. Winter is the driest season in Japan and even a lighted cigarette butt, if not carefully disposed of, may send blocks of houses up in flames. During the month of January, 1953 there were 354 fires in the city of Tokyo alone. Houses built of such flimsy materials are easily ignited. Arson is very widespread in Japan. Some people set fire to houses out of spite, while others do so in order to get the insurance money. In total disregard of the safety of others not a few Japanese resort to this utterly reprehensible act.

Fire-fighting equipment in Japan leaves much to be desired. But even a modern fire brigade would be utterly incapable of coping with the many fires that break out in the country, because the buildings are made of such combustible materials. In winter, when everything is so dry, usually by the time the fire engines reach the scene of a fire, it has reached

182

such proportions that it cannot be brought under control. Most Japanese cities are suffering from an acute housing shortage as a result of wartime destruction. Much effort has been expended to replace the dwellings, and there has been a mushroom growth in recent years of cheap wooden housing units. But during the winter months more houses are destroyed by fire than new houses are built.

It is remarkable with what nonchalance and fatalism the Japanese view this wholesale destruction of housing. I remember when I was a boy I used to go and watch fires in my neighborhood, for they were as frequent then as now. There was usually a curious crowd who congregated in the area to watch how swiftly the flames engulfed the houses. I am afraid that some even took secret delight in the impressive spectacle of the fire consuming one house after another. Among the milling crowd who gather in the area and thereby hinder the operation of the firemen, there are usually members of unscrupulous gangs intent on stealing any objects of value which might be salvaged from the scene of the fire. These people will scavenge around for anything left on the spot in the aftermath of a fire. The popular Japanese term "fire-thief" originally referred to such a gang, but the term now refers to one who fishes in troubled waters.

It is true that there have been at times outcries to remedy these lamentable conditions. The construction of fireproof buildings and the organization of more efficient fire-fighting systems and equipment have been suggested as possible solutions. But neither of these measures would be entirely effective. For one thing the Japanese would not build their houses with any materials other than wood. Japan has rich forests on account of its mountainous terrain and abundant rainfall. Some people maintain that Japanese forest resources were depleted during the war by indiscriminate cutting and that little effort has been made to replant them. This state of affairs only applies to certain parts of the country. In Fukushima, one of the largest prefectures in northeastern Japan, for example, only one-fifth of the timber resources has been tapped, mainly because of the inaccessibility of the area. Because more than 80 per cent of the total area of the country is forest land, lumber is still plentiful and is the only building material that can be procured comparatively cheaply and easily.

Japan has many kinds of wood of excellent quality, which accounts for the development, from early times, of wooden construction. She has, of course, some supply of stones, such as sandstone or volcanic rock, but they are less accessible than natural wood. Moreover, wooden buildings have always been favored, for, aside from other considerations, it is much more difficult to build with stone than with wood. Japanese dwellings of reinforced concrete, except for tenement houses for the poorer classes, have to be ruled out for ordinary purposes, because of the sultry summer weather and also because of the heating problem in winter. Besides, my countrymen prefer the single housing unit, with its garden, to an apartment house.

A few years ago there was an extensive fire in Atami, the celebrated seaside hotspring resort west of Tokyo. Some two hundred inns in the heart of the town were destroyed, and when I passed the devastated area by train the day after the fire, I saw the whole area levelled to the ground; the debris and litter presented a ghastly sight. When I passed through Atami again only a month later, I could see practically no trace of that fire; the area had already been built up with new wooden and stucco structures, and the town was bustling with activity!

Near Ueno Station, one of main railway junctions of Tokyo, is a street lined with wholesale candy stores. Thousands of retail merchants from nearby prefectures flock daily to this district, which is known as Candy Shop Alley. A few years ago there was a big fire which gutted three-fourths of the area within an hour or so. When I visited the area the next morning, the enterprising merchants had already constructed improvised stores of aluminum and tin, the stores were full of wares, and business was as brisk and animated as ever. This is no exaggeration, but the absolute truth.

Oddly enough, a big fire in Yedo, the old name for Tokyo, actually stimulated the growth of the city rather than harmed it. In the wake of the conflagration, movement of goods from various parts of the country suddenly became brisk, and men—carpenters, merchants, and speculators—all poured into

185

Yedo from outlying provinces and some even got rich on the profits made from materials needed for reconstruction. A story is told of an enterprising lumber merchant by the name of Kinokuniya Bunzaemon, who became one of the greatest parvenus that Japan has ever produced. He was a son of a lumber merchant in the province of Kii, in the southwestern section of the country. When in the early 18th century fire broke out in Yedo and reduced a large part of the city to ashes, Bunzaemon seized the first opportunity to go down to Kiso, the foremost lumber producing area of the country, long before the first news of the fire reached the province. He took a large number of gold pieces, which he gave freely to children playing in the streets in order to win the confidence of their parents. Soon, they all agreed to sell him a large amount of lumber, which he sent to Yedo on credit, thereby amassing a fabulous fortune. This episode is somewhat analogous to a legend that is told of the Rothchilds: how Nathan Rothchild flashed the first news of the imminent fall of Waterloo to London by means of relays of swift horses and a chartered boat across the English Channel, and there bought up all the British Government bonds that were available. He also made a fabulous fortune.

The speed with which the Japanese reconstruct areas destroyed by natural calamities is amazing. I visited Tokyo in 1926, three years after the great earthquake and fire. It was difficult to find traces of the holocast which destroyed almost entire sections

186

of the metropolis. Many of the German cities bombed out during the war had tremendous difficulties disposing of the voluminous debris, composed of steel, brick, and stones. No doubt the Japanese were luckier in this respect than the Germans, since the bulk of our buildings were constructed of flimsy wooden materials. Nevertheless, the speed with which the Japanese rehabilitate their devasted areas must be because they are so inured to natural disasters that they look upon the task of rehabilitation, however gigantic, as almost a part of their daily lives.

Kyoto is one of the few cities which the Americans spared from fire-bombing during the war, because of the numerous historic temples and shrines and valuable objects of art in which this ancient capital abounds. There was in Kyoto the Gold Pavilion, an exquisite temple with a gilded roof, built many centuries ago. Last year one of the junior monks in this temple, because of a grudge he nurtured against his chief monk, callously set fire to this historic monument and completely demolished it. The whole nation mourned the loss of the Gold Pavillion, which will never be duplicated.

A few days after this tragedy the aged mother of the culprit committed suicide in atonement for her son's unpardonable act. The monk's act is a typical example of callousness of the Japanese toward his obligation to the community in which he lives. The mother, on the other hand, was imbued with strong family consciousness. She felt that the disgrace her son brought on her and her family was so tremendous

187

that she could no longer bear it. However, she was concerned not so much with the harm her son's misconduct had done to society as with the sullied reputation of her family.

One often finds in Japanese homes and in toy shops a mascot called *daruma,* which represents a sort of roundish man with no legs and is usually painted in red. It is the Japanese version of Dharma, the Indian Buddhist saint of the sixth century, who is believed to have sat for years in meditation without stirring, until he lost the use of his legs. This mascot-toy is so weighted at the bottom that it remains upright even if knocked down. Merchants, desirous of financial prosperity, often use such a *daruma* as a mascot, for it suggests an undaunted spirit which is not put down by failure. If I am not mistaken, a similar mascot is known in the West as Billikin.

The natural disasters to which the Japanese are so often subject have gone far toward forming the character of our people. The absence of an abundance of fertile land and the occasional destruction of what little land they do have, either by typhoon or tidal wave, has made them industrious, though not necessarily energetic. They cannot survive, as do their Filipino neighbors, on the fruits of labor of a few days each year. There has always been the necessity of unremitting toil, much as with a swarm of ants assiduously building their nest and hauling provisions to it. Through centuries of comparative privation the Japanese have learned to survive by a maximum expenditure of energy on a minimum of clothing, food, and shelter. Above all, natural calamities of various sorts have ingrained in them an indomitable spirit as exemplified in the mascot-toy of *daruma*. "Seven falls and eight rises" goes a Japanese proverb. It means that one may fail seven times but will succeed on the eighth try, as long as one is imbued with an undaunted spirit.

It may be asked why the Japanese stick so tenaciously to their homeland, which offers so little in natural resources and moreover is so subject to the catastrophic vagaries of nature. The Japanese are not pioneers and possess little of that passion for exploration and development of virgin lands which has been such an important part of American history. They have not felt that lure of distant plains which in less than a century carried Americans through the natural dangers of forests and mountains and the marauding of hostile Indians all the way to the Pacific coast. In Hokkaido, the large northern island of the Japanese archipelago, there is still enough uncultivated land to take care of a few million of Japan's surplus population. Unlike other islands, Hokkaido is singularly free from the ravages of earthquakes and typhoons. In spite of all this, the island remains comparatively sparsely populated, for it has never been subject to any steady stream of immigration. The Japanese could have migrated to the virgin areas of Brazil and Argentina in large numbers. The government used to encourage emigration with subsidized passages and liberal bounties. Nevertheless, only about a quarter of a million Japanese found

189

their way to South America during the fifty years before the war. Manchuria tells a similar story.

Unlike the Chinese, the Japanese will not willingly go where there is either extreme heat or extreme cold. The Japanese did not migrate in any substantial numbers to Formosa, Korea, Manchuria, or the Federated Malay States. These places have been exploited by the Chinese, who had no better opportunities than did the Japanese. Other peoples, the Spaniards, British, French, Portuguese, Dutch, and Americans who sought and found greater opportunities for putting their energies to work, have gone into the undeveloped places of the world and made them blossom and produce.

The Japanese do not have that courage which has enabled other peoples to plunge into the wilderness and, by their own individual efforts, wrest a living from the soil. Three centuries of Tokugawa feudal government prior to 1868, during which period the country was hermetically sealed against the outside world, stifled whatever ambition or initiative the Japanese may have possessed. The people of Japan enjoyed comparative peace during the Tokugawa period, and the population was stabilized by various crude methods. They believed that theirs was a beautiful domain in which to live and learned to seek pleasure and enjoyment in small things. In due course, the Japanese lost their ambition and initiative for expansion, and have managed to live in a crowded country by intensive utilization of what little resources are available to them.

11   A Nation That Acts as One

FROM time immemorial the Japanese have been a most thoroughly ruled people. Likewise, there has never been a popular struggle for liberty or individual rights, as in France, England, or the Americas. The idea of the people being sovereign has never risen to obstruct the ambitions of rulers and courtiers, and it is but little understood even to this day. Many bloody battles recorded in Japanese history were fought to decide who would rule, but never to determine how those in power should rule. Great families have fallen and others have risen to power through the fortune of battle, but few struggles have ever been consecrated to a great principle, or for the vindication of a just cause. I do not believe that my foreign friends are aware of these facts.

Rulers have risen and fallen, and subjects have changed masters, but the relationship between the

191

two classes has never altered. The Japanese people have suffered oppressions which few other peoples have had to endure. In the Japanese Middle Ages, subjects were taxed to support civil warfare from which they would derive no benefits. The people were forced to pay oppressive taxes which enabled the ruling classes to live in idleness and luxury. At one period, in addition to the taxes on the produce of the land and on other forms of production, there was a forced labor tax of thirty days annually imposed on every male between the ages of twenty-one and sixty-six years and one of fifteen days on every minor. Still, these tyrannical exactions and heavy tax levies never drove the people to rebellion.

Our historical record is in striking contrast to American, British, or French history, where one is able to trace a slow but gradual development of personal liberties. The major events of Japanese history consist of nothing more important than a change of masters, some more oppressive, some less so, than their predecessors. The people have on many occasions taken up arms to aid their feudal lord in his petty warfare against a rival, or to promote his ambition of securing supreme power, but they have never struck a positive blow on their own behalf. This remarkable fact can be explained by the Japanese belief that whoever is at the head of the state, whether emperor or military dictator, is supreme and almighty—the source alike of sovereignty and morality—and therefore unassailable! Obedience to his commands and loyalty to him are the beginning and the end of Japanese morality. Having complied with these requirements the Japanese conscience is forever clear.

From the political point of view, equally important to the belief in the unassailability of whoever is at the helm of the government, is this Japanese conception of morality based on the idea of loyalty. It might even be said that the Japanese word for, "disloyalty" is the nearest synonym for the Christian concept of "sin." The moral absolute in Japan has always been loyalty—loyalty to emperor, to feudal lord, to husband, to parents, to family, or to clan.

Taking orders from superiors has thus become second nature to the Japanese. It is said, quite rightly, that the American Occupation of Japan was an astounding success, the like of which has not been recorded in the annals of military history. While credit must be given to General MacArthur and his benevolent policies, the extreme docility of the Japanese is largely responsible for the success of the Occupation.

A few years after the war Japanese trains were very crowded, and some people even rode on the locomotives, in defiance of the orders of the railroad officials. The officials put out a notice on the locomotives saying that riding on the locomotives was strictly forbidden "by order of the Occupation Forces." The prestige of the Occupation was enough to bring the unruly Japanese into line. Also during the hectic postwar period some people dumped garbage and refuse into the side streets of Tokyo, for the municipal garbage collection system was not functioning normally. Soon I noticed signs posted at many places which read: "Do not dump garbage here—by order of the Occupation Forces."

Since orders from superiors are inevitable, once the orders are issued there is no alternative but to obey them. There is no room for argument, for disobedience is unthinkable. Hence one sees notices everywhere in Japan which almost always take the form of orders, for example: "Don't walk on the grass," or "Don't sound horn in school zone." There are very few signs inducing the populace to voluntarily observe the regulation or soliciting the cooperation of the general public in civic matters, such as are often found in America or Britain, as for example in the "You have been warned" signs on the highways. In this respect Japan bears a close resemblance to Germany where *verboten* signs are ubiquitous.

When people are always told to do this or to do that, individual initiative is largely suppressed. It should also be mentioned that Japanese lack of initiative is partly due to the extreme congestion of the country. If in a crowded place everyone had his own way, people would be constantly bumping into each other. In a crowded subway all one has to do is to stand still and wait patiently until the train reaches the next stop. There is no room for independent action on the part of individual passengers to relieve the congestion. You are deprived of freedom of movement and thereby lose freedom of thinking. My opinions here may not follow with mathematical nicety, but I am confident that they reflect the psychological reactions of my countrymen.

I once built a California-style house with a spacious garden around it. Unlike most Japanese houses it had no fence or wooden walls around it. A swarm of neighborhood children would peep through the windows and spy on us while we were eating or doing other things. In no time at all the entire neighborhood was well informed as to our standard of living. On three occasions thieves broke into the house and stole many of my valuables. After that I hurriedly built hedges and walls around my house.

In overpopulated Japan, privacy is very hard to maintain. Everyone is subject to prying eyes all about him and is constantly exposed to the criticism of others. If anyone behaves a little bit differently from others, he is the object of considerable criticism. I once bought an American gas cooking-range, which no doubt was a luxury by the existing Japanese standards. Several people in my neighborhood happened to see the men delivering the range from a van into my house. That was fatal! In the matter of a few weeks everybody in the neighborhood, as well as in my office, knew about it. Since that time whenever I was asked to make donations or contributions, it was insisted that I should be able to make a larger one inasmuch as I was so wealthy as to own an American cooking range. That's Japanese psychology for you.

The Japanese cannot mind their own business,

largely because they live so compactly that their interests are closely interwoven. If, for example, an individual occupies more than the normal space for a house, the other eighty-eight million people would have that much less room. So they cannot be disinterested in what others are doing. They would kick up a row and criticize the individual in an attempt to dissuade him from occupying such a spacious lot.

In such an extremely congested country as Japan there will always have to be a certain amount of regimentation in order that the general welfare of all the people can be assured. The general public tends to act and think *en masse*, since there are so many individuals that consideration cannot possibly be given to individual desires or requirements. As a result of this social regimentation, the Japanese have learned to live together in their crowded islands with relatively few outward signs of friction. However, ambition is thwarted in the process and the Japanese tend to be petty in many things they do.

Some time ago a group of Japanese kindergarten children were invited to a tea party given by an American woman educator in her home in Tokyo. Each boy and girl—about a dozen in all—was given a bottle of Coca Cola and some cookies. Just then the telephone rang, and the hostess had to go and answer the call. She was further detained by someone dropping in to see her. She was gone for about fifteen minutes from the scene of the party. When she came back she found to her amazement that all

196

the little guests were still holding the coke bottles and cookies in their hands and that none of them had taken a drink or eaten a piece of cookie.

In the rearing of children in Japan great emphasis is placed upon the fundamental courtesies of life and upon respect and admiration for their elders. In the instance given above I am certain that the children were thinking of those teachings while their hostess was absent. Although some Japanese might not agree, it is my decided opinion that another Japanese character trait is also evidenced here. This is lack of initiative on the part of the Japanese. In situations like this it is particularly noticable. Unless someone gave the children a go-ahead signal and ordered them to eat the refreshments, they would not think of starting by themselves. At this party there must have been considerable discussion among the children as to whether or not they should start to eat their refreshments while the hostess was away. Since no decision was forthcoming, no one was brave enough to set an example and start eating, however tempting the refreshments might have been. If, however, one of them had started eating without waiting for the permission of the hostess, irrespective of what other children said or thought, then the rest of the group would undoubtedly have followed suit.

While on our tour of inspection of the United States, we were entertained royally wherever we went. We were very much impressed by the warm American hospitality. At many dinner parties we were offered drinks before dinner and were asked our choice. "Do you like bourbon or Scotch?" or "Do you like martinis or Manhattans?" were the usual questions. Members of my group would look helplessly at each other and reply, "Whatever you choose." I was sorry for the host or hostess for such procrastination, which must have seemed inexplicable. I felt that I should not keep the host waiting and so made it a point to give my choice before the others merely for the purpose of breaking the ice. The rest of the group invariably asked for the same thing I did. Incidentally, Scotch was my choice of whisky, and martinis my favorite cocktail; so I am afraid that many Americans got the mistaken idea that all Japanese prefer Scotch whisky to bourbon and martinis over Manhattans!

The Japanese people find it difficult to make up their minds on any question when the decision has not been predetermined by rule or precedent or by a superior. The majority of people have not been able to break away from tradition, and few have developed the ability for independent thought or action.

The remarkable unanimity of opinion on national affairs is not so much the result of patriotism, but because the people do not think about public affairs but merely blindly follow their leaders. For many years prior to the war, Japanese leaders exhorted the people to act as one. Japanese patriotism combined the highest motives of civic and religious duty, but differed from other patriotism in that it was characterized by narrow chauvinism and blind devotion on the part of the people to their leaders. In all the foreign wars that Japan has engaged in there has never been an anti-war party, let alone conscientious objectors. Such privation and misery as were forced upon the people during four years of the Pacific War would have driven a less docile people to revolution.

Because the Japanese are reluctant to take the initiative, there are numerous meetings and conferences held in Japan. Meetings are convened even for the discussion of trivial matters. These are usually attended by large numbers of people either directly or indirectly connected with the matter at hand, and discussion may continue for hours on end, with little likelihood of a decision being made. This may sound like a very democratic way of reaching a decision, but in truth it is not. As soon as someone takes a positive stand, the others present usually submit to his decision, and dissenting voices disappear. Consultation goes on until the moment someone takes the initiative, but once a decision is made, there is no more discussion.

In a country where individual thinking and independent action are practically nonexistent, everything is done *en masse*. Suicides have always been very prevalent in Japan. A forlorn and dejected person, instead of steeling himself to make renewed efforts, often chooses the easiest way out—suicide. In recent years, because of economic hardship, there have been many suicides. In fact a day seldom passes without newspaper reports of several such cases. In many instances the husband tries to persuade his wife and children to take their lives simultaneously and sometimes administers doses of poison to unwilling children. Besides family circles there are numerous instances of several friends committing suicide together when they find the outlook for the future hopeless.

Japanese schools conduct trips for their pupils to various places at least twice a year. These school excursions are a part of the school curriculum and are intended to show the pupils places of interest. The duration of these trips ranges from one day to several days, depending on the school grade concerned. On such trips no individual arrangements are permitted. Year after year Japanese railroad stations are thronged with such groups on conducted tours. Only in Germany have I come across similar group activities involving school children.

Marriage ceremonies are also sometimes conducted on a collective basis. Several couples go to a temple or shrine, where the wedding rites are performed simultaneously by one chaplain. This is done primarily for reasons of economy but also because many people want to get married the same time others do. Incidentally, June weddings are not popular in Japan. November is considered the best month for marriage, and many couples get married during that month.

In Japan, where people like to act collectively, even robberies are carried out in groups. Several

200

prospective robbers convene and embark on their nefarious undertakings together in order to embolden themselves and to overcome resistance.

This lack of initiative has given rise to uniformity of thought and action among the Japanese. University students wear uniforms and one can tell them from other people and also recognize the different universities by the distinctive uniform and cap that each is identified with. This applies to other schools as well, right down to kindergartens, and in the absence of special uniforms or caps, a school badge is used to show affiliation. Even government employees have office badges affixed to their lapels, so that everybody will know which establishment they work for. This outward manifestation of uniformity reflects the true mentality of the Japanese people.

Thus the Japanese people generally act and think *en masse*. And in the mass they are sometimes swayed in one direction by the trend of the times and then in another. Several years prior to and during the war the use of English was suppressed and German was encouraged. Everyone tried to learn German without regard to its usefulness. Today English is taught extensively throughout the country. Even in remote districts where no English-speaking person is ever likely to show up, shops have signs in English. The avidity and zeal with which the people are studying English today is sometimes comical and occasionally pathetic. And these are the same people who tried to master the German language with equal zeal only a decade ago.

201

Along with uniformity, the unrealism of the Japanese people is something which the student of the Japanese people should always bear in mind. The Japanese tend to accept and apparently at least be satisfied with a nominal state of affairs, which may be quite different from actual conditions. The theoretical solution of a question is accepted without reference to the real facts. As a result, the Japanese are often unable or at least refuse to distinguish between theory and fact, or between phantasy and reality.

For instance, most Japanese believe, to some extent quite justifiably, that the scenery of our country is so superlatively beautiful that many foreign tourists want to visit Japan. Japanese officials embark upon publicity campaigns to encourage foreign tourists and recently designated some remote mountain areas as "national parks." However, these officials have never given serious thought to building decent motor highways or to improving hotel accommodations.

Inducement of foreign capitalists to invest in Japanese enterprises in order to rejuvenate the shattered economy of the country has been a theme often harped on in recent years by statesmen and business leaders alike. However, these advocates of foreign, particularly American, investment, have done almost nothing to make it worthwhile for American capital to seek investment in Japan. In particular, the Japanese hoped that Americans would invest in hydroelectric power projects. Whenever an American engineer visits parts of rural Japan our newspapers herald the event as a preliminary to impending American investment. The truth of the matter is that there are few undertakings at present which hold forth the promise of immediate returns on American investments, and, incidentally, a hydroelectric project is one of the least attractive enterprises in this respect.

The Japanese indulge in wishful thinking in many things. Before embarking on the Pacific War Japanese jingoists propagandized intensively for "Asia for Asiatics." The militarists ran amuck in various Asiatic countries during the war and subjected innocent native people to privation and even torture. Still, they hoped that all Asiatics would rally to the banner of "Asia for Asiatics." This is a typical example of Japanese naiveness, which confuses theory with reality.

Japanese Shinto shrines have what are called *mikoshi*, or portable shrines, which are miniature replicas of the shrines themselves about the size of a sentry box. At the annual festival of the shrine volunteers from the neighborhood, usually husky young men numbering anywhere from a dozen to several scores, carry this portable shrine on their shoulders and march along the street. At the start of the demonstration the shrine-bearers are usually quiet, as though taking part in a funeral procession. As they go along, however, they become more and more vociferous, until a kind of frenzy takes hold of them. Soon this gang of husky young men start tossing the shrine into the air, and the whole show gains in momentum, amid a wild uproar and maddening din. They then forget themselves, and the whole group acts as one, with a feverish enthusiasm. They might even go to the extreme of tossing the shrine into a nearby store and smashing the windows in order to give vent to a grudge they have against the storekeeper. The procession then becomes uncontrollable and the young men, fired by the frenzy of youth and in the ecstacy of the festive mood, turn into veritable madmen.

During the Pacific War, Japanese army personnel were often charged with acts of brutality. Some of these cases were no doubt exaggerated, and some people even believe that the Japanese, who by nature are so quiet and timid and not prone to brutality, could not have perpetrated such crimes.

The Japanese, however, are capable of doing unbelievable things if gotten together under a certain kind of leadership. This is exactly what happened at Pearl Harbor and during the subsequent catastrophic war. No sane Japanese would have imagined his country waging a war, let alone winning one, against the formidable array of the Anglo-Saxon powers. Yet the Japanese people, whipped to a frenzy by the military clique, did go to war, and nobody in Japan could stop the nation once it had started on this fateful march, any more than a group of anxious bystanders could stop the wild progress of a portable shrine being carried on the shoulders of a maddened crowd of young men.

12 "Apres Guerre"

HOWEVER misty the beginnings of Japanese history may be, there is no doubt that the Japanese empire is one of the oldest in the world. According to traditional chronology the present Emperor is the 124th descendant of Emperor Jimmu, who ascended the throne in 660 B.C. to become Japan's first ruler.

During its long history there is only one recorded instance of the Japanese islands having been seriously threatened by aggression from abroad. This was the abortive Mongol invasion in the 13th century. Kublai Khan of the powerful Mongol Empire wished to subjugate Japan and in 1274 sent a strong Mongol force, which succeeded in landing in northern Kyushu. Before any serious engagement took place the enemy forces decided to withdraw because of extreme weather conditions which threatened their fleet. They came back in 1281, this time with a formidable armada, and once again landed in northern Kyushu. The invading forces— 150,000 strong—were equipped with superior weapons and gunpowder. The Japanese were greatly outnumbered, and the situation seemed almost hopeless when, as luck would have it, a typhoon descended on the fleet and annihilated it, bringing this large-scale invasion to a catastrophic end.

The Japanese called this typhoon *kamikaze,* or divine wind. They thought that their land was protected from foreign invasion by the will of the gods. This incident has loomed large in Japanese historical tradition and instilled in the minds of the people an irrational conviction that their country was sacred and invincible.

During the Pacific War, the Japanese Air Force sent out squadron after squadron of reckless suicide pilots against enemy concentrations. These men were called *kamikaze* pilots. The Japanese High Command, by sending out these ill-trained but determined and dedicated pilots, hoped against hope that another divine wind might arise unexpectedly to frustrate enemy invasion, just as in the Mongol invasion seven centuries before.

Apart from this Mongol episode the Japanese have never suffered an armed invasion throughout their long history. Like England, Japan's insular position afforded ample protection from foreign foes. The straits between Japan and Korea, the nearest point on the continent, are well over 100 miles wide, many times the width of the Strait of Dover. Petty local warfare among feudal lords and clans was almost continuous up to recent centuries, but these were of no consequence as far as national unity was concerned. During the nation's long, hermit-like existence, much was done to strengthen the popular belief in the divinity of the Emperor. The continuous progress of Japan after the Imperial Restoration of 1868, when the country was opened for foreign intercourse, only served to augment this fiction of divinity. Two foreign wars, first against China and then against Russia, were fought in the name of the Emperor, and as a result of participation on the side of the Allies in the First World War, Japan acquired territory and wealth. Commerce, manufacturing, and shipping expanded at a remarkable rate, and Japan came to occupy an important place in the family of nations. The Japanese gave credit for all of these accomplishments, not to the men who were responsible, but to the virtue of the Emperor and to the guardian-spirits of their divine ancestors.

Japan could never have grown as powerful as she did without some ideal to lure her onward. This imperialistic ideal was the only one available. It gave remarkable solidarity to the Japanese people and was the lever that raised Japan from Oriental impotence to a high place among the great powers of the world.

Japan had never known defeat at the hands of a foreign enemy. Some hotheaded Japanese before the war even went so far as to assert that it was the manifest destiny of Japan to rule over all of Asia. I doubt whether anyone who had travelled about the world and been any kind of an observer believed such things.

It must be obvious how such a highly-united people, firmly indoctrinated in the belief in the divine mission of their country, would react to such a catastrophe as defeat in war. Just as a towering tree is knocked down by a violent storm, so Japan lies prostrate today. Japan was vanquished for the first time in her history, and came under the direct control of foreign conquerors.

In Europe and on the Asiatic continent, where wars, both great and small, have been fought among various neighboring countries from time immemorial, nations are used to the fortunes of war and consider either victory or defeat as but a link in the chain of historical events. This is particularly true in Germany and France and perhaps in England too, considering the centuries of British colonial expansion and contraction. With them postwar demoralization and stupor are comparatively short-lived. I know the case to be quite the contrary in Japan.

It is a fact of great significance that all Japanese had been led to believe in their nation's invincibility. Fantastic as it may sound, there are still quite a few Japanese in Brazil who refuse to accept the fact of Japan's defeat. No quantity of recent Japanese newspapers or books sent to enlighten these people in Brazil has been able to convince them of Japan's surrender. Also, nine years after the war, groups of Japanese stragglers are still found from time to time in the South Sea jungles. Most of these hold-outs refuse to believe in their country's ignominious defeat until they are actually brought back to Japan.

Despite a degree of outward economic recovery, Japan is still in a turmoil. Our eighty-eight million people are leading peaceful lives under American protection. But they are like so many sheep who have lost their shepherd. The Japanese nation, such a closely-knit unit before, is now disintegrated. It was popularly said of the Chinese that they could be likened to a pile of sand and that the Japanese could be likened to a lump of clay. The Japanese of the postwar period are no longer a piece of clay but a pile of sand. Our eighty-eight million people are groping in the dark for something—perhaps divine inspiration, or leadership, or anything that will make them become cohesive again. As individuals the Japanese are weak, forlorn, and aimless.

After the war, State Shintoism, an emperor-worship cult, was outlawed by the Occupation authorities, and Buddhism lost in popular favor. Various sects of Christianity have gained a large number of followers, but these still represent only a small minority among the total population. On the other hand there has been a mushroom growth of dubious cults, many of which border on absurdity and superstition. Most of the newly-created cults have won millions of devout followers and are flourishing, which shows that there was a large spiritual vacuum created as a result of defeat.

As is the case with most other countries the

postwar period in Japan has been characterized by moral laxity, expecially among the younger generation. Japanese youth has reacted sharply against rigid wartime regimentation. What is preached as democracy is often taken by them to mean that they are now free to do anything they please. Not having recovered from the stupor of crushing national defeat and with little thought to the future, they merely seek transient pleasures and material gain and nothing else. Lewd literature is avidly read and sexual behavior has become extremely loose, compared with before the war. Postwar economic difficulties have driven some youths to commit the most daring crimes, and juvenile delinquency is widespread.

The French words *après guerre,* after the war, have been widely used by the Japanese since the war. To say that a person is an *après guerre* means that he dresses ostentatiously and devotes himself to pleasure-seeking, little mindful of his obligation to the community. An *après-guerre* businessman may be described as a shrewd operator who built up his business by shady, black-market deals during a brief period, but whose continued prosperity is somewhat problematical. A college student can also be an *après guerre*. He frequents dance halls, passes examinations by hiring a proxy, and may engage in unorthodox money-making activities. In any event an *après guerre* denotes an unsavory character, a bad influence on others, and a person given to pursuing his own selfish ends.

In postwar Japan many resident foreign nationals have also been *après guerre*. During the war foreign residents had little freedom, and their activities were closely watched by the police. As soon as the war was over foreigners in Japan suddenly became a privileged class. They were given special food rations by the Japanese government at a time when the Japanese themselves were almost starving for lack of rice. Scarce items like fresh butter, eggs, and meat were sold to them at nominal prices. Moreover, foreigners, including Germans and other ex-Axis nationals, were allowed to hold foreign currency, when possession by the Japanese of a few U.S. dollars was severely punishable by the Occupation authorities. With such privileges it was not difficult for any foreign resident to make a fortune, unless he was a hopeless imbecile.

A certain foreigner living in Kobe was in dire straits during the war years. As soon as the war ended he started hawking butter, cheese, sugar, and other specially-rationed items to other foreigners and to the Japanese at exorbitant prices. A year or so of such petty blackmarketeering enabled him to accumulate a little capital. He changed the money he made into U.S. dollars with which he bought imported foodstuffs to again sell illegally to the Japanese. At that time Japanese courts did not have jurisdiction over foreigners, so he was free to do whatever he wanted. In due course he started buying for nominal sums real property which had been requisitioned by the Occupation Forces from their Japanese owners. The American Occupation Forces in Japan appropriated

211

various houses, office buildings, and land, and the Japanese government was directed to reimburse the owners of such property from the Japanese budget. The owners received only nominal payment, which was little better than outright confiscation. Furthermore, the owner could not even be hopeful of its eventual restitution, should the Occupation drag on for years. Under the circumstances landlords were inclined to part with their property while it was still under requisition, if there was a buyer for it. The foreigner mentioned above bought up at least a dozen fancy villas and a few substantial office buildings, while they were still being used by the Americans. He then did his best to persuade the American Occupation authorities to release some of the buildings, and he was partly successful in this attempt. He is now a wealthy man, having gone into the import-export business with extensive operations in various business centers throughout the world.

Several Far Eastern fortunes were made by foreigners in postwar Japan. At the time that Japan was still closed to foreign trade immediately after the surrender, foreign traders flocked to Japan, and, by obtaining licenses from the Occupation authorities to export Japanese manufactured goods, they could squeeze competing Japanese exporters, who were totally ignorant of overseas market conditions. Japanese manufacturers, not having direct access to foreign markets, had no alternative but to do business with these foreign traders, who did a highly lucrative business. Such abnormal situations no longer exist.

Another successful *après guerre* was a Japanese. He was one of the first to meet the vanguard of the American Occupation Forces who landed at Yokohama a few days after the surrender. This man opened a small money-exchange booth on the pier and sold Japanese yen to thousands of incoming American officers and soldiers in exchange for dollars. Of course in those early days there was no restriction against the Japanese holding American currency. This enterprising Japanese also bought cigarettes from almost every American, as they were in great demand among the Japanese people, and sold them at a tremendous profit. Another undertaking of his on the Yokohama pier was to sell cheap Japanese bric-a-brac, such as bronze Buddha images, brass candleholders, and incense burners, which he had salvaged from bombed-out areas. Being great novelties in those days, these curio items sold like proverbial hotcakes. He was able to make a handsome fortune from these three enterprises—transactions in greenbacks, cigarettes, and junk. When the regulation was enforced against Japanese possessing greenbacks, he bought a Chinese passport from local Chinese sources and legally become a Chinese citizen, and therefore an Allied national. He was then free to deal in U.S. dollars, and the outcome of his manifold business activities was that today he is one of the few prosperous businessmen in the country, a typical *après guerre,* still only in his thirties.

It is not fair to apply the stigma of *après guerre* to Japanese youth alone. One finds them in almost every strata of the population. The majority of the older generation, however, are apathetic. Imperial princesses, statesmen, and business magnates who knew better times during the heyday of the Japanese Empire now talk wistfully of the past and behave as though Japan were still a first-rate power in the world today. These people are unable to face stark reality and are too proud to join in the cutthroat struggle for existence that has characterized life after the war. Burdened with heavy taxes and inflation, they are fast being reduced to poverty and eventual extinction as a class. The term *shayo-zoku,* or "sunsetting class," an expression of postwar vintage, aptly describes this type.

The younger generation of Japan today should not be entirely despaired of. Aversion to war is most pronounced among Japanese youth. They look back on their wartime service as recruits in the fighting services as so much wasted effort. They are ashamed for having allowed themselves to be blindly exploited by the military. The majority of them want no more of war. Hatred of war is particularly intense among young ex-servicemen. Although they have no lofty goals to work toward, a stabilized, richer, and more respectable—if commonplace—life is their ultimate aim. Still, Japanese youth find even these modest desires hard to fulfill. Postwar economic difficulties force them to exert all their energies just to make a living. Students are particularly hard-pressed, as 90 per cent of all college students have to work their way through school. The large number of American students who find it necessary to work their way through school have little in common with their Japanese counterparts. In terms of ease and lucrativeness the odd jobs American students take to pay for their school expenses have no parallel in Japan. Japanese college students peddle peanuts on the streets; they walk as sandwich men along the main thoroughfares, defying the sneers and stares of their friends and acquaintances; they operate shady businesses, and pose as nude models for painters. In fact there is no job under the sun which Japanese students will not do, provided it fetches the equivalent of fifty cents a day. Even white-collar salaried men with respectable and steady employment in business or government have to do something on the side in order to make a decent living.

Nevertheless, Japanese youths, like their fathers and grandfathers, are inarticulate and feeble as individuals and practically incapable of independent thought. In the absence of a fixed ideal or conviction, they will jump at anything that appears novel and attractive. It is impossible to change the inherent characteristics of a people overnight. The youth of Japan will readily respond to leadership if a strong leader emerges again.

If, despite all their efforts, Japanese youth find they cannot attain even a modest living, they will be terribly disillusioned. There no longer exists the divine inspiration that motivated youth before and during the war. In actual fact emperor-worship or ancestor-worship were religions themselves. Apart

215

from offering homage in temples and shrines, the Japanese take their indigenous religion lightly. For instance, there is no set day of worship as in Christianity. Japanese would pray before a Shinto shrine dedicated to ancestor-worship or in a Buddhist temple. But I must say that whatever their own faith, they showed the greatest respect for the faith of others. Hundreds of thousands of shrines and temples throughout Japan served as a bulwark of faith for the people who cherished them as links between themselves and the myriads of deities to whom they are dedicated. This vague ancestor-worship has long been a national religion for the Japanese. Deprived of these forms of worship they now have nowhere to turn for spiritual solace.

Communism in Asia is not like communism in Europe. The doctrine and the goal may be the same, but the reasons people are attracted to it are almost entirely different. In Europe, communism is an answer to frustrations which are more often spiritual than physical. It is an interpretation of history which provides a satisfactory alternative for those who no longer accept the will of God.

In Asia, communism is by and large the direct result of poverty. The most fervent Communists are not necessarily the poor themselves, but those who are disgusted by the corruption and injustice which poverty produces. The masses are generally docile and fatalistic and readily respond to leadership. In Asia, the permanent basis for revolution is that it is steadily getting poorer. The consequent loss of all hope for a better future makes men ready to take desperate action.

Discontent is spreading in Indo-China, Malaya, Indonesia, and Burma because of extreme poverty. It is not only that wider and wider classes of the population are awakening to the misery of their lot; unless there is economic equality also, poor countries will remain corrupt countries, always offering fertile ground for communism.

Postwar Japan fulfills both of these conditions; and spiritual frustration, coupled with widespread poverty, presents a dangerous situation.

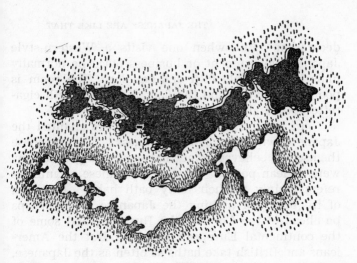

13   The Two Japans

IT is probably the experience of every foreigner who has resided in Japan for any length of time to find so many contradictory elements in practically every phase of Japanese life that he is often baffled. Every generalization, whether in favor of Japan or against it, can be disproved by an overwhelming mass of contradictory evidence. One can find evidence that the Japanese are industrious, lazy, efficient, incompetent, kind, cruel, peaceful, or warlike.

When visiting a Japanese house or restaurant one is struck by the immaculate matted floors and the perfect symmetry and simplicity of the interior

219

decoration. But when one visits a Western-style Japanese government or business office he normally finds indescribable filth and squalor. The room is poorly ventilated, and the floor is littered with cigarette butts and wastepaper.

In prewar years foreign observers credited the Japanese with personal cleanliness. The Japanese themselves believed somewhat conceitedly that they were a clean people. However, Japanese cleanliness refers mainly to their daily bath habit. In terms of frequency of bathing the Japanese may perhaps be ahead of the Chinese, the Russians, and some of the continental European peoples. But the Americans and British take baths as often as the Japanese, and their bathroom facilities are more sanitary than Japanese ones. As for public health and sanitation generally, Japanese standards are something to be ashamed of. A ride on a Japanese train will convince anyone of how indifferent the Japanese are to public health measures. Passengers throw cigarette butts and matches in the aisles; the car is permeated with the acrid smell of orange peels, discarded lunch boxes, and other refuse and litter, and soon looks like a garbage heap. The lavatory likewise gives off foul odors, which are often wafted into the car. Still no one bothers to clean up the place, and even if a member of the train crew sweeps the aisle, it does not take long before the car once again looks like a pigpen.

Japanese politeness, too, is often commented upon by foreign observers. If a stranger asks the way, a polite and obliging Japanese will walk blocks out of his way to direct him. After calling on other people the Japanese apologize most profusely for "taking up too much of their time, thereby causing not a little inconvenience." A Japanese bus conductor will address every passenger, when the latter is about to get off the bus, with "many thanks for your patronage." Yet Japanese policemen or petty officials are often very rude and insolent to those whom they are supposed to serve.

Japan is indeed a land of many contrasts. As the result of war the country is pauperized. Millions find themselves in dire economic straits. Many people develop a fatalistic attitude akin to despair. In fact not a few people commit suicide because of economic difficulties. On the other hand Japanese restaurants and plush teahouses are thronged nightly with business executives and others who do not seem to think twice of spending millions of yen on entertaining and revelling.

There is little philanthropic work undertaken by the wealthy. Despite the fact that there are so many needy college and university students requiring scholarships, compared with Western countries, few weathy people offered financial help even in the relatively prosperous prewar years.

A traveller to Japan cannot fail to notice rice paddy fields being carefully worked throughout the country. Japanese farmers in early summer transplant rice saplings from nursery beds; they take minute care when transplanting these young plants.

221

Rows and rows are planted with exact precision, without the use of tools. It is remarkable that such precision and symmetry can be attained by human hands. On the other hand, when visiting a Japanese business or government office it is disgusting to see how disorderly clerks allow their papers and documents to become. A petition presented a few days before may have been mislaid and cannot be located, or can be found only after an intensive and thoroughgoing search. The Japanese have not learned Western filing systems, and their filing is unscientific and unsystematic and most disorderly. An uneducated farmer can perform wonderfully systematic work in his rice paddy, while an office worker does not have a rudimentary idea of how to maintain office files.

It is not generally known that during the war the Japanese Navy possessed the largest aircraft carrier in the world. This was the "Shinano," a monster warship displacing 72,000 tons with full load. She was the mightiest carrier that ever sailed the seas. She bristled with the finest weapons and was fitted with the most up-to-date equipment. The Japanese Navy also had the two super-dreadnaughts, "Yamato" and "Musashi," each of 64,000 tons, the largest battleships ever built by a modern navy. Despite such outstanding achievements of the erstwhile Japanese armed forces, one witnesses inefficiency and lack of manual skill even in the use of the most primitive tools. There are few good paved roads in Japan, with the exception of two or three roads running out of the capital city of Tokyo for a distance of twenty or thirty miles. One wonders why the Japanese, who could build such super-dreadnaughts as the "Shinano," cannot or will not build a paved highway between the two principal cities of Tokyo and Osaka, a distance of a mere three hundred and fifty miles.

Visitors to Japan are often surprised to find how punctually Japanese trains run. Tokyo-Osaka express trains, for example, run according to schedule almost to the second. Stopovers at principal stations are usually timed at thirty seconds and are observed almost infallibly. Nowhere else in the world have I seen trains run with such exacting punctuality. Similarly, factories, schools, and banks keep punctual hours. I have seen many customers being refused admittance to a bank when they arrived one minute after 3 P.M., the usual closing time for banks. However, in keeping business and social appointments the Japanese are exceedingly lax. They seem nonchalant and do not even apologize for being ten or twenty minutes late for an appointment. They do not realize that they are breaking a rule of common etiquette. Unpunctuality is particularly common in rural districts, where the pressure of time is not as great as in the cities.

Despite their poverty the Japanese are a wasteful people. In Japanese offices employees use stationary lavishly and throw whole sheets into the wastepaper basket without making full use of them. Despite a critical paper shortage, the supply of stationary in Japanese offices is almost as abundant as in American offices. When water faucets are left running or leaking in public places, the Japanese seldom take the trouble to turn them off. The average Japanese does not think of turning off lights when they are not needed, although the shortage of electricity is a big hindrance in Japanese industrial expansion. Although the Japanese are poor, many of them do not pay much attention to small money, whether change from a purchase or a coin dropped in the street. This contrasts strongly with China, where not a single item of any value is wasted. It is said that seagulls do not follow Chinese steamers going in and out of the port of Shanghai, as no garbage is ever thrown into the sea by the frugal Chinese.

Thus, Japan is a land of paradoxes and extremes, of great wisdom and great stupidity. This contradictory state of affairs is accounted for principally by the great differences between different classes of people, differences in development which have produced rather sharply contrasted results. There is, for example, official and unofficial Japan. Official Japan, made up of the ruling oligarchy, having the first demand on the brains of the country, is comparatively efficient, progressive, and, in outward appearance at least, governed by the same code of morals that governs similar classes in other countries. Unofficial Japan, the Japan of the people, is still largely bogged down with feudalistic ideas.

In the matter of cleanliness, for instance, well-to-do and well-bred Japanese usually dress neatly, keep their homes spotlessly clean, and having probably travelled abroad, know what the standards of sanitation in a modern country should be. Country folk, on the other hand, have never seen the outside world and have no idea whatsoever of modern sanitation. They do not particularly mind if the odor of their lavatory permeates their living quarters, or if their children do not keep their nostrils clean.

In Japan striking contrasts are found between urban and rural areas. Downtown Tokyo is a city of wide thoroughfares and of many enormous steel and reinforced concrete buildings, resembling cities in Europe or America. In Osaka and other major cities also there are many modern office buildings and schools of steel and concrete, and one sometimes wonders if these are really cities of the Orient. In country places, however, thatched farm houses and small paddy fields, ox-drawn carts and honey-bucket wagons forcibly remind one of the centuries-old traditions of Japanese rural life.

Likewise, the difference in living standards between city dwellers and rural inhabitants is far greater than in America and Europe. For this reason, many Japanese, once having lived in Tokyo and becoming used to the modern amenities of city life, hate to go back and live in their native provinces. Similarly, ambitious and intelligent youth prefer not to stay in their provincial homes but strive to go to Tokyo and make their careers there. Serious efforts have been made since the war to decentralize the Japanese government, but I am skeptical of the success of these efforts. The best brains always prefer to stay in Tokyo.

There is a Japan of the East and a Japan of the West. The Japanese are perfectly at home in the Japan of the East. Their temples and shrines, for example, are exquisite architecturally and defy imitation by any other people. When a Japanese builds a Western-style house, however, it is often left unfinished or made ridiculous in its final details. Similarly, the majority of Japanese have not yet learned how to use Western rooms and buildings. A floor, unless covered by *tatami,* or straw matting, is considered an extension of the sidewalk, and as such they think they can throw cigarette ashes and even half-lit matches on it with impunity.

The Japanese may enjoy eating Western food, but they eat Japanese-style meals of fish, rice, and pickles with greater relish. In Japan foreign-style restaurants are well patronized during the lunch hour but less so in the evening. The Japanese prefer to relax on the matted floor and enjoy their native food at night. I have known many Japanese who, having been abroad and becoming accustomed to Western breakfasts, cannot go back to boiled rice and thick bean soup for breakfast. However, those Western-ized Japanese who formed the habit of eating toast and tea or coffee in the morning still prefer Japanese meals for lunch or dinner.

A Japanese may dress in Western clothes during his working hours, but once at home he removes his shoes, changes into kimono, and sits on the floor.

Unfortunately, East and West do not blend harmoniously in Japan. Everywhere one finds the East and West clashing with each other, and the result is often chaos and confusion. The culture of present-day Japan is a strange conglomeration of undigested borrowings from Western civilization mixed with many elements surviving from feudal ages.

The Japanese are very fond of hanging Western paintings in their homes. They hang heavy Western-style oil paintings in delicately constructed Japanese rooms of paper and sliding doors. It simply ruins the decorative motif of Japanese architecture and is an artistic malapropism.

Business offices in Japan are similar to those in New York or London. Yet the Japanese do not have proper janitorial service, and instead of sweeping the floor they often spray water on it to settle the dust. The window glass is left uncleaned for months on end, but no one seems to mind. It just does not occur to them to clean the glass. Such appalling negligence, however, is due to the fact that Japanese are used to paper screens, which they replace when the paper becomes soiled or torn.

Because the West has proved superior in many things, the Japanese live a dual life and have indiscriminately borrowed as much from the West as possible. However, the Japanese have not been able as yet to blend and harmonize Western and Eastern

227

ways of living. The same holds true of their mentality and behavior. The Japanese are generally considered a polite people. Yet their traditional politeness is often a veneer, except in the case of well-bred people. Their politeness is, if anything, aloof and pompous and does not comprise thoughtful consideration of others, the basis of good manners in the West.

I am often encouraged to think that if the two Japans could ever be made into one harmonious Japan, it could be a combination of what is best in our native culture with the best of the West. It is surprising how many tens of thousands of Japanese have travelled abroad before and since the war. After the Imperial Restoration of 1868 a large number of Japanese were sent abroad by the government each year to study Western institutions. Later, with the expansion of foreign trade, Japanese businessmen travelled in increasing numbers to every nook and corner of the world. These people naturally come home with new ideas and with an insatiable desire to reform their own antiquated country. However, they constitute a small minority in a nation of 88 million people, and their efforts are soon frustrated in the face of such overwhelming odds. Human inertia is such that these Japanese, at first full of enthusiasm upon their return home, in due course succumb to the preponderance of feudalistic ideas and antiquated practices.

This dichotomy of the two Japans will disappear when one Japan, progressive and liberal, emerges victorious over the other Japan, feudalistic and inefficient. At the moment the old Japan still seems to hold sway over the new. Yet this power of inertia is bound to diminish as more and more Japanese are given opportunities to learn about the outside world.

I cannot express adequately my conviction in this matter, now that the Occupation has come to an end. Since the surrender on 2 September 1945 at least half a million Americans, Britishers, Dutchmen, Frenchmen, and other foreigners have resided in Japan. Their mere presence, not to mention their words and actions, no doubt exercised a salutary effect upon the Japanese. Millions of Japanese had never seen Westerners before in their lives. The American Military Government taught the Japanese. how to run their government in a democratic way, and my countrymen for their part were quite responsive.

Since the end of the war thousands of Japanese have visited foreign countries, notably the United States. The orientation program run by the Department of the Army has enabled a large number of representative Japanese to see at first hand how American democracy operates. All the members of the mission which I took to the United States were profoundly affected by their detailed study of state and municipal governments, administrative boards, and commissions. Their meeting with responsible and friendly American officials and administrators will have lasting significance. Some Japanese feared that

229

Americanization or foreignization of Japan might be the result of the Occupation. The Americanization of Japan would mean the end of the Japanese nation as it exists today and would necessitate a reconstruction much more difficult than that which Japan underwent for half a century after emerging from seclusion. In my opinion this Americanization or foreignization is neither probable nor possible. Japan will not be threatened by the influx of a large number of foreigners, who would either purchase land or set themselves up in competition with native workers. Now that the military occupation is over, it is improbable that foreigners will remain in Japan in large numbers, for my country offers few opportunities for them. No doubt ten or so of the largest cities will again have their foreign colonies. Most of these are foreign residents needed as executives and staffs for the various importing and exporting concerns. However, most Americans will want to seek their opportunities not here but in the United States. Few will stay here as outright owners to manage their own enterprises. Perhaps these will number a few thousand.

Remarkable progress was indeed made during the Occupation toward the creation of a peaceful and democratic Japan, but there is no assurance that progress toward this end will continue to be rapid or even steady. What the future holds in store for Japan will depend in large measure on the success of cooperation with other countries of the world. The Japanese must eat. They have to sell their products in order to eat. Furthermore, I must repeat that the Japanese people have qualities which impede rather than accelerate democratization in the Western sense. Certain people entertain misgivings as to whether the Japanese are strong enough to endure the long period of economic hardship that lies ahead without falling prey to some radical political philosophy.

Despite many such uncertainties I feel reasonably confident that the Japanese people in time will succeed in blending East and West. Today they are groping in the dark. It will take time before they can completely recover from their postwar stupor.

From the late 6th century until the early 9th century there was a period of intensive learning from China, which was then at the height of its civilization. The Japanese acknowledged the superiority of all phases of Chinese civilization over their own and assiduously copied almost everything Chinese. In due course they assimilated these borrowed manners and institutions into their own and created the basis of contemporary Japanese culture.

Thus the Japanese are an adaptable people. In the past they have proved themselves capable of abandoning old customs and habits of thought once they were aware of something better. When the leaders of the Meiji Imperial Restoration of 1868 realized that their feudal system was no match for the Western parliamentary system, they made a startling about-face and did away with feudalism. It is quite possible that Japan will make another about-face

No one can tell what the new age in Japan will eventually turn out to be—democracy or authoritarianism, liberalism or communism—but it will be the Japanese people themselves who will forge their destiny.

C. FELT